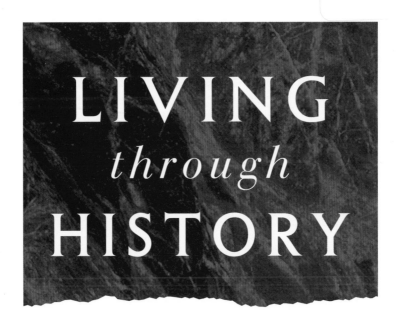

LIVING *through* HISTORY

Foundation Edition

Medieval Realms

Fiona Reynoldson
and
David Taylor

Heinemann

CONTENTS

Chapter 1	**1.1**	This is medieval England	4
Chapter 2	**2.1**	Why was England invaded in 1066?	8
	2.2	William v. Harold 1066	10
	2.3	King of England?	12
	2.4	A new way of ruling?	14
	2.5	What were early Norman castles like?	16
Chapter 3	**3.1**	Power over people's minds	18
	3.2	How was the church organised?	20
	3.3	Pilgrims and holy days	22
	3.4	Fountains Abbey: beginnings	24
	3.5	What did the monks do all day?	26
	3.6	Nuns and nunneries	28
Chapter 4	**4.1**	Who will rule?	30
	4.2	Henry II, law and order	32
	4.3	Church v. State: the murder of an archbishop in 1170	34
	4.4	Crown v. Barons: King John and Magna Carta 1215	36
Chapter 5	**5.1**	What were the crusades?	38
	5.2	The Siege of Acre 1189–91	40
	5.3	How did the Third Crusade (1189–92) affect England?	42
Chapter 6	**6.1**	What was a medieval village like?	44
	6.2	Cuxham: who did what?	46
	6.3	Cuxham: the Manor Farm	48
	6.4	Cuxham: patterns of life	50
	6.5	Village crimes	52

Chapter 7	**7.1**	What happened in Wales, Scotland and Ireland?	54
	7.2	The first settlement of Ireland	56
	7.3	Taking over Wales	58
	7.4	Losing Scotland	60
Chapter 8	**8.1**	Medieval towns	62
	8.2	Lincoln: mayors, markets and guilds	64
	8.3	Southampton: merchants and trade	66
	8.4	What was it like to live in a medieval town?	68
Chapter 9	**9.1**	The Black Death – a world-wide plague?	70
	9.2	How did people react to the plague?	72
	9.3	The Black Death at Cuxham	74
	9.4	How did the Black Death affect other places?	76
Chapter 10	**10.1**	The Peasants' Revolt 1381	78
	10.2	What happened in Suffolk?	80
	10.3	Treachery and death at Smithfield!	82
Chapter 11	**11.1**	The Hundred Years' War: Edward III and the Battle of Crécy 1346	84
	11.2	The Hundred Years' War: Henry V and the Battle of Agincourt 1415	86
	11.3	The Wars of the Roses: York v. Lancaster	88
	11.4	Richard III – the last Plantagenet king of England	90
	Glossary		92
	Index		93

1066	1100	1150	1200	1250	1300	1350	1400	1450	1500

The medieval period

The twentieth century

1900	1950	2000

The Middle Ages

The Middle Ages lasted for over 400 years.

The Middle Ages started in about 1066 and ended in about 1485.

The phrase 'Middle Ages' has been made up by historians as a label for this time in history.

The Middle Ages are also known as medieval times.

Life in the Middle Ages

- Rich people had lots of time to enjoy themselves (Source A).

- Poor people had to work very hard (Source B and Source C).

- Most people prayed a lot to God (Source D).

Source A

A picture from a book made about 1410. Rich people are out hawking. Hawks were used to kill smaller birds.

Source B

What a medieval person said about poor women.

If the baby cries in the night, the women have to get up and rock the cradle.

They have to darn and wash clothes.

They spin wool to earn more money. But still they have not enough food to feed the children.

The women often go hungry.

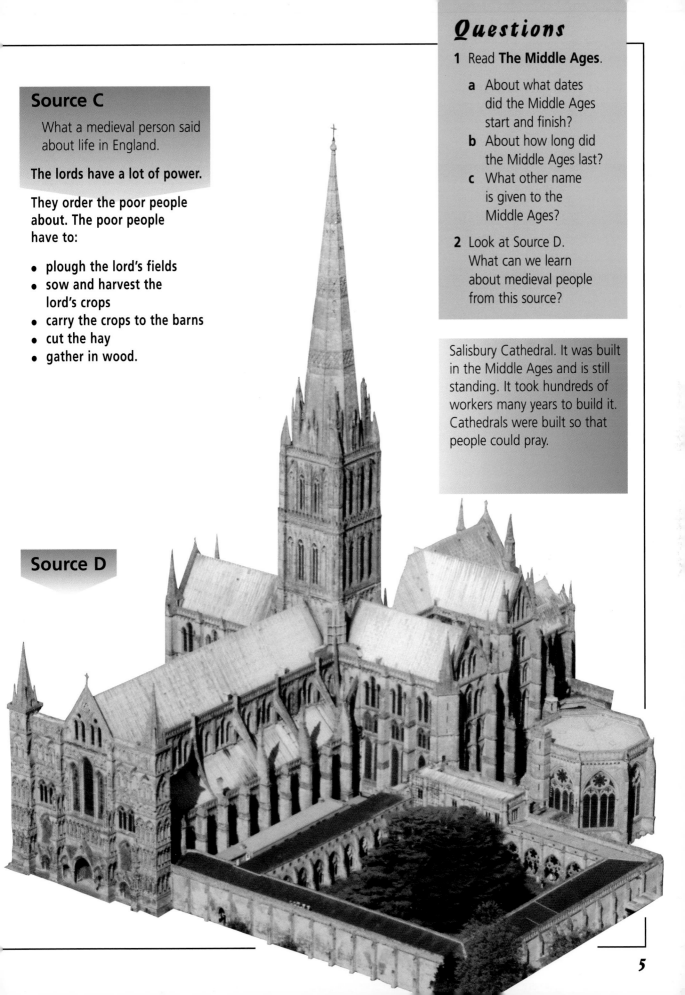

Source C

What a medieval person said about life in England.

The lords have a lot of power.

They order the poor people about. The poor people have to:

- plough the lord's fields
- sow and harvest the lord's crops
- carry the crops to the barns
- cut the hay
- gather in wood.

Source D

Questions

1 Read **The Middle Ages**.

   a About what dates did the Middle Ages start and finish?
   b About how long did the Middle Ages last?
   c What other name is given to the Middle Ages?

2 Look at Source D. What can we learn about medieval people from this source?

Salisbury Cathedral. It was built in the Middle Ages and is still standing. It took hundreds of workers many years to build it. Cathedrals were built so that people could pray.

5

Who had power in the Middle Ages?

The king ruled England.

The **nobles** also had a lot of power. They were rich enough to have their own armies.

If the king was strong, the country was peaceful.

Henry II (1154–1189) was a strong king. He kept law and order. He controlled the nobles.

If the king ruled badly, the nobles tried to get more say in the running of the country.

King John (1199–1216) was not liked. The nobles argued with him.

They made him sign the **Magna Carta** in 1215, which gave the nobles more power.

Source E

The king and the Church

- The **Pope** was in charge of the Church.

- The Pope lived in Rome.

- He told the bishops and priests in England what to do.

- Sometimes the King of England and the Pope fell out.

A king is crowned. Will this king get on with the Pope?

6

Wars against France

During the Middle Ages, English kings captured land in France.

The English and the French fought many wars.

The most famous war was the Hundred Years' War. It was fought between 1337 and 1453.

In the end, the English lost nearly all the land they had captured in France.

Heaven and Hell

People believed that bad people went to Hell.

Hell was a place where bad people burned for ever.

People believed that good people went to Heaven.

People thought that God decided who went to Heaven and Hell.

This was why they prayed a lot. They wanted God to think they were good.

Find out more!

This chapter has told you a little about life in the Middle Ages. The rest of this book tells you more about:

- who ruled the country
- town life
- village life
- wars
- the Church.

Read on!

Questions

Look at Source F and read **Heaven and Hell**.

1 What did people in the Middle Ages think Hell was like?

2 Why did people pray a lot?

A painting showing what medieval people thought Hell was like.

Source F

King Edward the Confessor died in 1066. He had no son to become king.

The next king?

Three men wanted to be King of England:

- Harold Godwinson
- Harald Hardrada, King of Norway
- William, Duke of Normandy.

HARALD HARDRADA, KING OF NORWAY

His father was promised the throne by an earlier king

A good fighter

EARL HAROLD GODWINSON

English

Promised the crown by Edward in 1066

A good fighter

NORWAY

N

S

ENGLAND

0   200 miles
0   300 km

NORMANDY

WILLIAM, DUKE OF NORMANDY

Promised the crown by Edward in 1051

He was Edward's cousin

His wife was related to an earlier king

Harold Godwinson had sworn to help William become king

A good fighter

Whom did Edward choose?

Harold   **Edward**   **William**

Pictures from the Bayeux Tapestry. The first picture shows Harold promising to help William be king. The second shows King Edward dying. By his bed the English earls are persuading Edward to choose Harold.

Harold as king

Harold was on the spot when King Edward died. He was crowned king. This made William and Harald Hardrada very angry. Harald Hardrada came to England with a big army. But King Harold defeated him in a battle. Now King Harold had to face William.

Source B

September 1066: Harold and William ready to fight.

Questions

1 Read **The next king?**
   Write down the names of the three men who wanted to be king.

2 Look at the picture on page 70.

   a Where did Harald Hardrada come from?
   b Where did William come from?

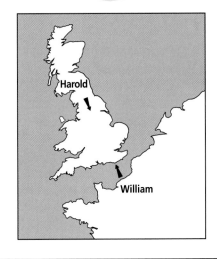

9

Source A

A modern picture of the Battle of Hastings drawn by Jason Askew this century.

William lands in England

William and his army landed in England in September 1066. They were called **Normans** because they came from Normandy. They marched to Hastings and waited for Harold there.

Harold marches south

Harold was in the north of England when William landed. So he got his army together and marched south to meet William.

On 14 October 1066, Harold reached Hastings. He was ready to fight William.

The Battle of Hastings 1066

Harold set his army up on a hill near Hastings. The hill was called Senlac Hill. William was in the valley below.

The battle begins

At 9 o'clock in the morning, William attacked. The battled raged all day.

Was William dead?

During the battle, someone said William was dead. His soldiers were terrified. But William lifted his helmet. He was all right.

Harold on the hill

Time and again William attacked Harold. But Harold and his soldiers stood firm on top of Senlac Hill.

The end of the battle

Slowly William's soldiers broke through. Harold and his best soldiers were surrounded. Harold's brothers were dead. Soon Harold was dead too. He was hacked to pieces.

Source B

The Bayeux Tapestry is the earliest source about the Battle of Hastings.
It was made between 1076 and 1086.
This picture shows Harold being killed.

William had won

William had won the Battle of Hastings. But could he win all of England?

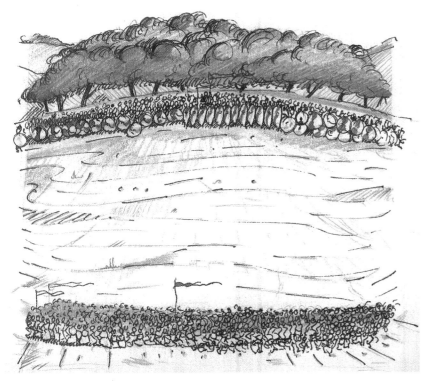

A drawing of Senlac Hill with Harold's soldiers on top and William's soldiers below.

Questions

1 Look at Source B.

  a What is the earliest source about the Battle of Hastings?

  b When was it made between?

  c What does this picture show?

2 Look at Source A.

  a When was it made?

  b Make a list of all the things that are the same in Source A and B. There are at least five.

William is crowned king

William won the Battle of Hastings. He marched to London. He was crowned king on Christmas Day 1066. But William still needed to take control of England.

William burnt villages

William wanted everyone to know he was king. He sent his soldiers into the countryside to make people obey him.

The soldiers burnt people's animals, food and homes. Many people starved to death.

William built castles

William had to make sure that he kept control. He told the Normans to build castles.

These castles dominated the villages around them. They showed people how powerful the Normans were.

William told the Normans to build strong stone castles to dominate the villages.

Source A

The Bayeux Tapestry shows William's soldiers taking villagers' animals in the top picture. They are burning a village in the bottom picture.

William took land from the English

William took land away from the English earls. Any earls who stood against him were killed.

William gave land to the Normans

William gave this land to his Norman friends. But they only kept it as long as they helped William.

William got control of England.

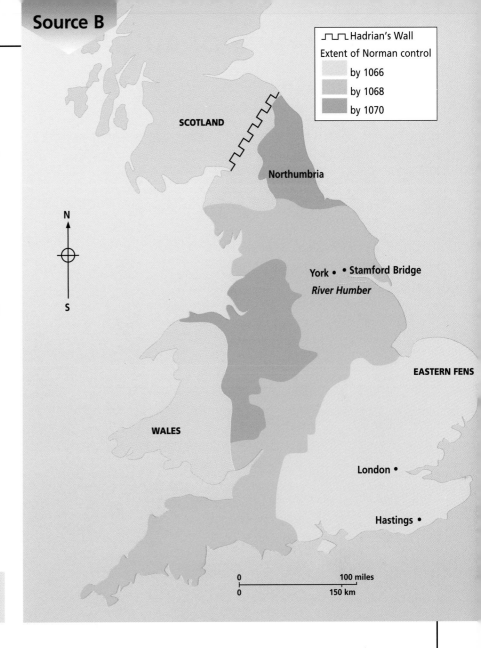

Hadrian's Wall

Extent of Norman control
by 1066
by 1068
by 1070

SCOTLAND

Northumbria

N

S

York • • Stamford Bridge
River Humber

EASTERN FENS

WALES

London •

Hastings •

0   100 miles
0   150 km

DOMVS:IN CEN DITVR:

Questions

1 Read **William is crowned king**.
   When was William crowned king?

2 Look at Source A.

   a What are William's soldiers doing in the top picture?
   b What are William's soldiers doing in the bottom picture?

2.4 A NEW WAY OF RULING?

Ruling England before 1066

Earls were powerful men. They owned a lot of land and helped the king to rule.

After 1066

William did not trust the earls. He took away their land.

William said he owned all the land. He gave it to his Norman friends. But he could take it back too.

Source A

William took land from an English earl. Here William is giving it to his own son-in-law, Alan. Alan is swearing to help William.

The Domesday Book

William wanted to know what England was worth. In 1085 he sent men to every village. They asked:

- the name of the village
- how much land it had
- how many people lived there
- how many ploughs it had
- how many mills it had.

The answers were made into a book called the **Domesday Book**.

The King

gives lots of land to

give loyalty and soldiers to

Norman Lords and Churchmen

gives some land to

give soldiers or money to hire soldiers to

Norman and English knights and earls

gives a house and a garden to

work for or give rent to

Peasants and Tenants

How the **feudal system** worked. ▶

WALTHEOF THE ENGLISH EARL

Waltheof was an English earl. He fought William fiercely, but William won. Then Waltheof swore to help William.

Waltheof was a good soldier. So William was pleased. William gave his niece, Judith, to Waltheof as a wife.

But Waltheof plotted against William again. William was furious and threw Waltheof into prison. Waltheof swore that he was innocent. Then the Vikings invaded in 1075.

Waltheof's wife said that he had told the Vikings to invade. William had had enough. He had Waltheof beheaded in 1076.

Who did William give the good jobs to?

This is a list of some of the bishops of Winchester. The word 'de' shows that the name is Norman. Richard is also a Norman name.

1007   Brithwold

1015   Elfsimus

1032   Alfwine

1047   Stigand

1070   Walkin

1100   William de Giffard

1129   Henry de Blois

1174   Richard Tocliffe

1189   Godfrey de Lucy

1205   Peter de Rupibus

1243   William de Raleigh

Questions

1 Read **After 1066**.

  a Did William trust the earls?
  b What did he take away from them?
  c What did William say?

2 Read **Who did William give the good jobs to?**
Write down the date of the first Norman Bishop of Winchester.

How do we know?

There are no early Norman castles left now. So how do we know what a Norman castle looked like? Here are some of the ways:

- the Bayeux Tapestry
- other pictures from Norman times
- books from Norman times
- bits of castles dug up from the ground.

Source B

A monk wrote this description of a castle around 1100.

The castle is on top of a big hill.

From the castle you can keep watch over all the land around it.

The keep is a tower with a wall around it.

The walls of the tower are very high.

You get to the keep by a bridge.

Source A

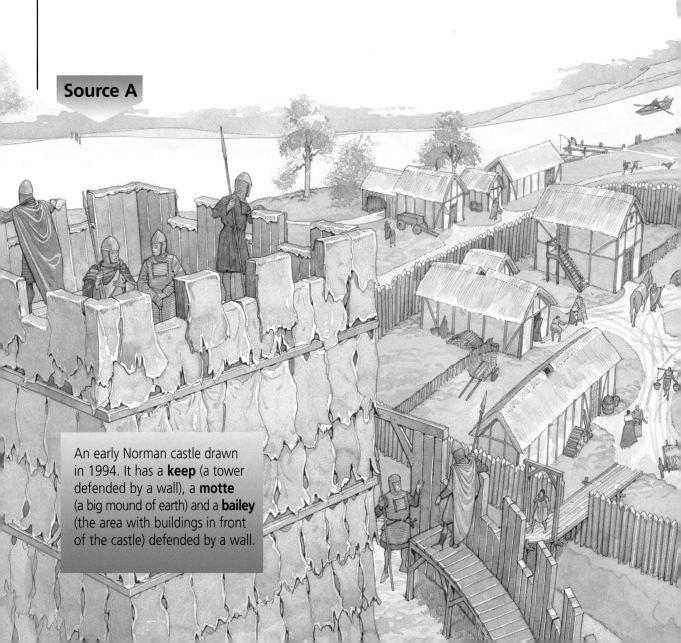

An early Norman castle drawn in 1994. It has a **keep** (a tower defended by a wall), a **motte** (a big mound of earth) and a **bailey** (the area with buildings in front of the castle) defended by a wall.

A battle from the ▶ Bayeux Tapestry. You can see a castle and its motte in the picture.

Source C

Source D

Some early Norman castles were made of wood. Some modern historians have been trying to find out more about wooden castles.

It is difficult to find out about wooden castles. They have rotted away. Sometimes the rotten wood leaves marks in the earth. Then you can see where they have been.

Questions

1 Look at page 16.
List four ways in which we can tell what an early Norman castle looked like.

2 Look at Source C.

   a Find the motte.
   b Find the keep (castle).
   c Find the steps leading to the motte.

3 Look at Source A. Write down 3 things that are different from Source C.

Christians belonged to one Church

All Christians believed in Jesus Christ. They belonged to one Church. The Church was led by the Pope. He lived in Rome.

The Church was powerful

The Church was rich and powerful. It owned a lot of land.

Most churches had wall paintings. They told a story. This painting shows St Michael. He is wearing a red cloak. He is weighing people's souls. He wants to see if they are good enough to go to Heaven. The devil is waiting to take the bad people to Hell.

Death

Life was hard in medieval times. Many adults died. Many children died. They died from plagues and other diseases. Sometimes they died from cold and starvation.

Heaven and Hell

But the Church said there was hope. Good people went to Heaven when they died. It was wonderful in Heaven. But bad people went to Hell.

What was Christendom?

Christendom was the part of the world where Christians lived. This was most of Europe.

Source A

Jerusalem

The most important city for Christians was Jerusalem.

They called it the Holy City. They did not want infidels to own it.

What was an infidel?

An infidel was what Christians called anyone who was not a Christian.

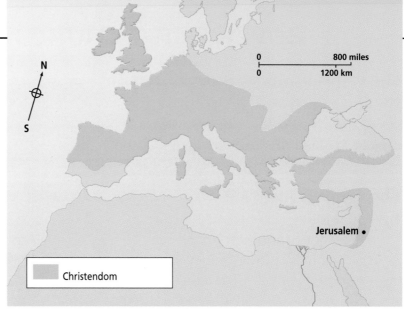

Christendom in about 1200.

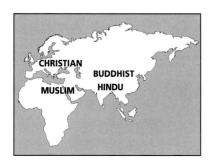

This map shows some of the religions of the world.

Source B

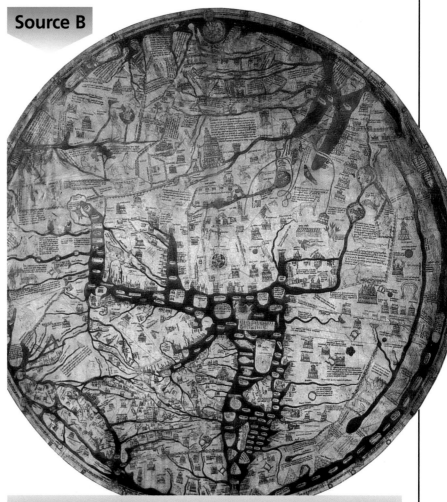

A map of the world drawn in about 1200. It shows Jerusalem at the centre of the world.

Questions

Read **Christians belonged to one Church**.

a What did Christians believe in?

b Who led the Church?

c Where did he live?

The Church was well organised

The Church was well organised. Look at the picture. You will see that the Pope was the head of the Church. He had lots of people working for him.

The Church was rich

The Church owned a lot of land. Sometimes kings and rich people gave the Church land or money. Over hundreds of years the Church got more and more land and money.

Rich people and Heaven

Kings and rich people gave land and money to the Church because they wanted to do good. Then they would go to Heaven when they died.

The Church and ordinary people

The Church had hundreds of priests. They worked in every village. The priests told the people about Christ and the Church. They told them about Heaven and Hell. They made people think about these things.

The Church and schools

The Church ran schools. So many churchmen could read and write, and were well educated. Kings wanted these men to work for them as well as for the Church. This was all right until the kings argued with the Church.

Source A

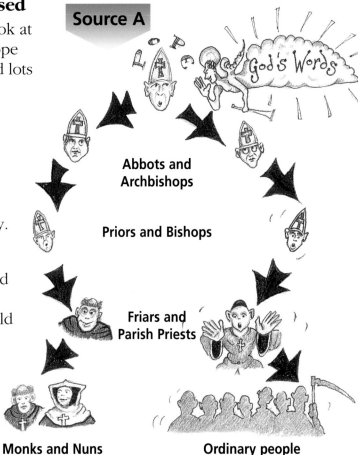

Abbots and Archbishops

Priors and Bishops

Friars and Parish Priests

Monks and Nuns

Ordinary people

This shows how the Church was organised.

The king was powerful. The Church was powerful. They often argued.

Priests

Most villages had a church and a priest.

Pray for the dead

Read and write (write letters for village people)

Farm his own land

Give food to the poor

Take church services

Collect Church taxes from people in the village

Keep records (write down births, marriages and deaths)

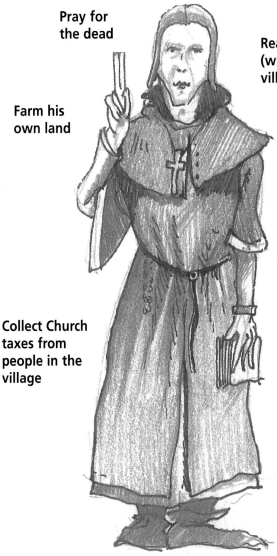

The priest's work.

Questions

1 Look at Source A.
Who was head of the Church?

2 Read **Priests** and look at the picture.
Write down the jobs the priest did.

WILLIAM DE KESTEVENE

William de Kestevene was a parish priest.

The picture below shows what he looked like.

When he was young, he worked for the king. Then he became a priest.

Most priests were poor. But William came from a rich family.

He left money in his will so that a brass picture would be made.

The picture was put up in the church when he died.

Pilgrims and pilgrimages

A pilgrim was a person who travelled to a holy place. The trip was called a **pilgrimage**.

Where did they go?

Some pilgrims travelled to Jerusalem. Some travelled to Rome. Some travelled only to a holy place in Britain. One holy place in Britain was Canterbury.

Why did they go?

Some people were sick. They went to a holy place and asked God to make them better. Other people wanted to thank God for helping them.

Some people went on a pilgrimage as a break from everyday life. They wanted to spend time thinking about God.

The holy places and relics

The holy places might be big churches. Often these churches had a **relic**. A relic was a bit of a saint or holy person. This might be a finger or a lock of hair.

Source A

The Canterbury Tales is a long poem about pilgrims going to Canterbury. It was written by Geoffrey Chaucer. This is one of the pilgrims.

Source B

This badge was worn by pilgrims who visited Canterbury.

Relics

A relic was a part of a saint's dead body, or something that had belonged to a saint. People believed these things were very holy.

Relics were important. If a church had a hand or some teeth from a famous holy person, lots of pilgrims would come to that church.

Holy days

The Church said that some days were holy days. These were days like Christmas and Easter.

Holy days were holidays. People went to church. Then they might celebrate with dancing or singing or seeing a holy play.

Plays and processions

Holy plays were put on in towns. The stage was a painted cart. The big churches put on processions. All the priests dressed in their robes and carried banners. They went all round the town. Then there was a feast and a bonfire.

Source C

Pilgrims gave money or something special to a holy place. Here are a few of the things given to Hereford Cathedral in August 1307:

- **450 gold rings**
- **70 silver rings**
- **108 walking sticks**
- **1,200 wax eyes.**

Thomas Cantilupe was the saint at Hereford. Pilgrims prayed for his help. They left all sorts of gifts at his tomb.

Questions

1 Read **Pilgrims and pilgrimages**.
 What was a pilgrim?

2 Look at Source C.

 a Write down the things that show people were asking for help with walking or giving thanks for walking better.
 b Write down the things that were going to make the cathedral richer.

3 Read **Relics**.

 a What was a relic?
 b Why were relics important?

Source D

Shepherds dancing at Christmas time. Taken from a manuscript made in the 15th century.

York Abbey in 1132

York Abbey was a big monastery. The monks had to live by the strict **Rule of St Benedict** – no speaking, and lots of work and praying.

By 1132 the monks did not live by these rules any more. They had lots of land and money. They lived a comfortable life.

Some monks rebelled

Some monks rebelled. They said they wanted to go back to the Rule of St Benedict. Other monks said no. They liked the comfortable life.

Archbishop Thurstan

Archbishop Thurstan arrived at York Abbey. He found the monks fighting. So he took away the monks who wanted a stricter life. He gave them some land to build a new abbey.

Source B

From the Rule of St Benedict.

- **All monks must work in the kitchen.**
- **All monks must work on the farm or in reading prayers.**
- **A mattress, a blanket and a pillow is enough bedding.**

Source A

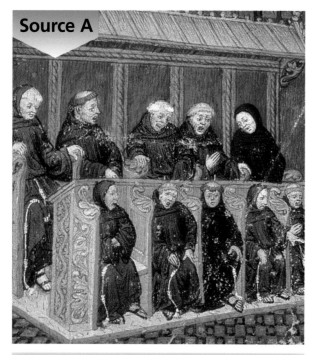

A painting of monks during a church service.

Source C

This is a description of where Fountains Abbey was built.

The land was thick with thorns. It lay between mountains.

Here the monks made shelters to keep off the harsh winter.

They worked to build a small church and to grow food to eat.

The artist has painted Fountains Abbey as he thinks it looked in the 1400s.

Source E

A modern photograph of Fountains Abbey in North Yorkshire.

Questions

1 Read **York Abbey in 1132**.

  a What was York Abbey?
  b What did the monks have to live by?
  c What was the Rule of St Benedict?

2 Read Source B.

  a What sort of work did the monks do? Find three sorts.
  b Write down the three pieces of bedding a monk was allowed.

Many monks

By 1300, one person in every 200 was a monk. The monks lived together in **monasteries**. They did many jobs:

growing vegetables · praying

keeping animals · reading

cutting wood · writing

cooking · cleaning

building · growing herbs for medicine.

Monks' clothes

Monks at Fountains Abbey wore woollen habits or robes. Each monk had:

1 habit (robe)	1 belt
2 cowls (hoods)	1 tunic
2 pairs of slippers	a knife
2 pairs of boots	handkerchiefs
2 pairs of blankets	needles
several pairs of socks	things to write with

Source A

The monks made beautiful books. Sometimes they copied out old books. Sometimes they wrote history books or books about medicine. They painted pictures in the books too.

Historians are not sure how the monks' habits (robes) were made. The monk below has a tunic over his habit.

cowl

habit

tunic · slippers

A monk painted this picture. It shows the monk in charge of the wine cellar. Some monasteries made wine.

The Rule of St Benedict said that monks must not speak. So they used sign language. Here is one of the signs.

This sign meant a person who had been killed for believing in Jesus Christ.

How the monks lived at Fountains Abbey

At first, the monks were very poor. They built a small church. Then they started a small farm and kept sheep. The years went by and they kept more sheep.

Then they built a big monastery. This was called Fountains Abbey.

Fountains Abbey grows rich

Rich people wanted to show they loved God. They gave money to the Abbey. The monks also made a lot of money from sheep farming.

Soon the monks were rich. They liked a comfortable life. Like the monks at York Abbey, they too began to forget the Rule of St Benedict.

Questions

1 What does Source B show?

2 Look at Source A.

   a What did the monks make?

   b What sort of books did they write?

3 Read **Monks' clothes**.

   a What were the monks' habits made from?

   b What tells you that the monks did their own sewing?

3.6 NUNS AND NUNNERIES

Monks and nuns

A **monk** was a man who wanted to serve God. A **nun** was a woman who wanted to serve God. There were fewer nuns than monks. Most women got married or worked as servants.

Why did women become nuns?

Some women did not want to get married and have children. Nuns learnt to read and write. They also learnt to run a big organisation. Some women liked this better than being wives and mothers.

Nunneries

The places where nuns lived were called **nunneries**. Many nunneries were poor because rich people gave more money to monasteries than to nunneries.

Nunneries changed

At first, nuns were well educated. They knew French, Latin and English.

But by the 1400s this had changed. Bishops said the nuns knew only English. Even worse, the nuns did not work hard for God any more.

Source A

JULIAN OF NORWICH

Julian of Norwich was a holy woman. She lived in a tiny hut by St Julian's Church in Norwich. That is how she got her name.

No one knows her real name.

She was born in about 1342 and lived poorly and simply.

She had many visions and she wrote about them.

One of the things she wrote was:

All will be well and all manner of things will be well.

She trusted in God to make things right.

Look at this painting. In the top row, a nun is pulling the bell rope. This is calling the nuns to church. This nun was also in charge of repairing the church building. The abbess is holding a crook or crosier. She was in charge of all the nuns. Another nun is holding the keys to the wine cellar.

A comfortable life

Over the years, the nunneries became richer – just like the monasteries. The nuns got used to a comfortable life. This was like the monks at Fountains Abbey.

The records of some nunneries show that the nuns spent money on parties at the New Year. They had May Day games and paid actors to put on plays for them at Christmas.

A nun going on a pilgrimage to Canterbury in the 1300s.

Source B

Nuns often helped in hospitals, or looked after travellers.

Source C

A modern historian writing about nuns in the 1400s.

Nuns wore golden hairpins and silver belts.

They kept pets. Dogs were the favourite pets, but nuns also kept monkeys, rabbits and birds.

They sometimes took animals to church with them.

Questions

1 Read **Monks and nuns**.
   What was a nun?

2 Look at Source B.
   What jobs did nuns often do?
   Find two jobs.

What the king had to do

Be a good judge in a law court

Lead his army into battle

Ride on horseback all over his kingdom

Keep control of the earls

Man or woman?

Most people thought that a man should be king. They thought women were not strong enough.

When Henry I died, he left only one living child. This was a girl called Matilda.

There was trouble ahead.

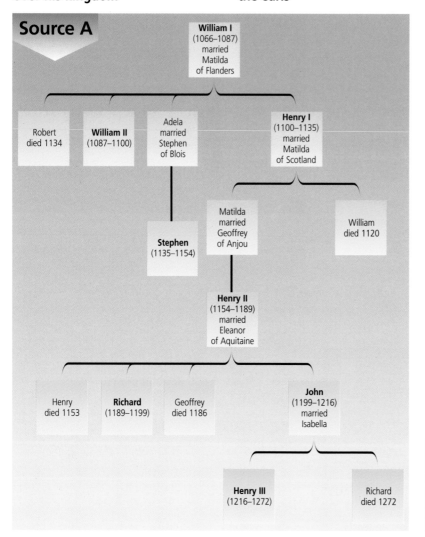

Source A

Family tree of English kings.

The dates in brackets are the years they reigned.

William I
(1066–1087)
married
Matilda
of Flanders

- Robert
died 1134
- **William II**
(1087–1100)
- Adela
married
Stephen
of Blois
- **Henry I**
(1100–1135)
married
Matilda
of Scotland

Stephen
(1135–1154)

Matilda
married
Geoffrey
of Anjou

William
died 1120

Henry II
(1154–1189)
married
Eleanor
of Aquitaine

- Henry
died 1153
- **Richard**
(1189–1199)
- Geoffrey
died 1186
- **John**
(1199–1216)
married
Isabella

- **Henry III**
(1216–1272)
- Richard
died 1272

Question

Look at **What the king had to do**.

Write down the four things the king had to do.

MATILDA V. STEPHEN

Henry I had two children – William and Matilda.

William drowned in 1120.

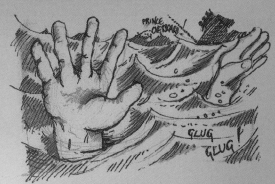

Henry made the earls swear to help Matilda.

Many earls did not want a woman to rule. They made Stephen, the king's nephew, king.

Source B

From the Anglo-Saxon Chronicle, 1137. This describes England when Stephen was king.

The earls filled the country full of castles.

They used the castles against the King.

Questions

1 Look at Source B. From reading this, do you think Stephen was a strong king or a weak king?

2 Read **What happened next?** What did Stephen agree with Matilda?

What happened next?

Matilda and Stephen fought for fourteen years. In the end Matilda gave up. But Stephen agreed that Matilda's son would be the next king.

How did Henry get his empire?

Anjou from his father

Normandy from his mother (Matilda)

Henry II

Aquitaine from his wife

England from his cousin (Stephen)

Find the places on the map on page 33.

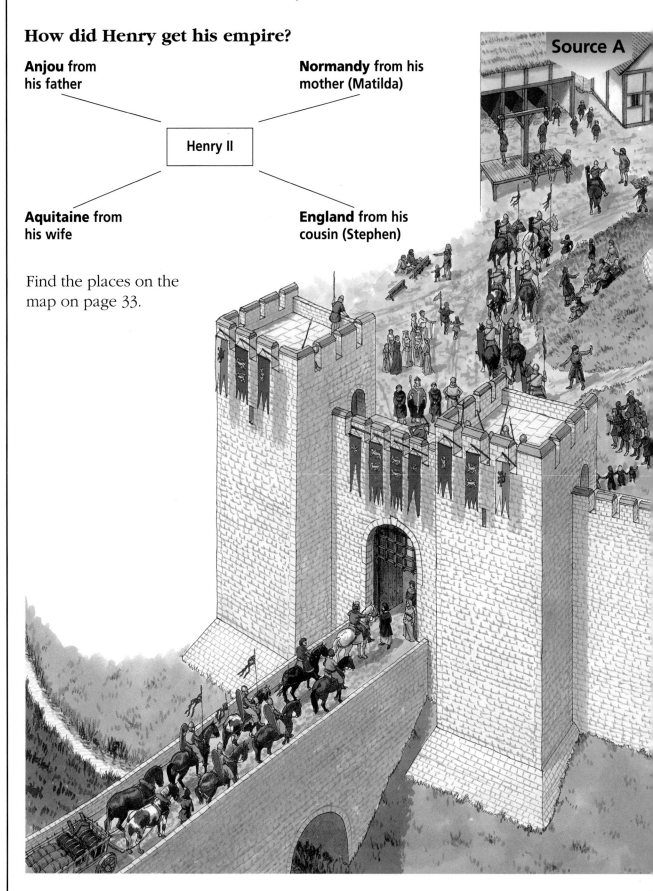

Source A

Putting the problems right

The war between Matilda and Stephen caused lots of problems.

When Henry II became King of England in 1154, he wanted to put these problems right. He wanted to make sure he was a strong king.

This is what Henry did:

- He had all new castles pulled down.
- He sent all foreign soldiers out of England.
- He took back all the land that Stephen had given away.
- He asked the earls for money so that he could pay an army.
- He set up law courts and judges. Sometimes Henry was a judge himself.

Source B

From a letter written by Henry's secretary.

Although his legs are sore from hard riding, Henry never sits down.

Often he gets up in the middle of the night and sets off somewhere. Men run about like mad and pack horses are loaded quickly.

Questions

Look at Source A.
What is going on in the castle? Choose from the list below:

1 Children playing
2 Men watching TV
3 Men in the stocks
4 Women talking
5 Men being hanged
6 Women hanging out washing
7 Soldiers on guard
8 People cooking
9 People carrying food
10 Soldiers fighting

Henry II and his followers ride to Orford Castle, in Suffolk.

The King is going to be a judge at one of the courts there.

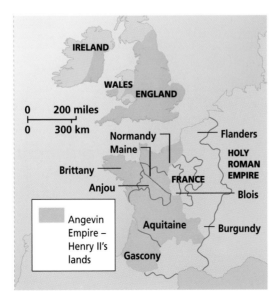

IRELAND

WALES

ENGLAND

0   200 miles

0   300 km

Normandy
Maine

Flanders

HOLY ROMAN EMPIRE

Brittany

FRANCE

Anjou

Blois

Angevin Empire – Henry II's lands

Aquitaine

Burgundy

Gascony

Henry II's empire.

Henry II wanted control

When Henry became king, he wanted to control three things:

- He wanted to control the earls.
- He wanted to control the law courts.
- He wanted to control the Church.

The Church and the king

The Church was very strong. It had its own law courts. Henry hated this and thought of a clever plan.

He had a great friend called Thomas Becket. He would make Thomas head of the Church in England. Then he would control the Church.

But Thomas said no. He told Henry that, if he was head of the Church, then the Church would come first.

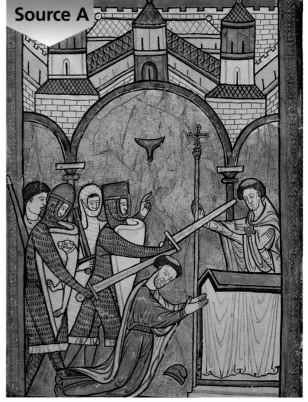

Source A

This picture of the murder of Thomas Becket was painted in about 1200.

Thomas Becket becomes Archbishop of Canterbury

The king did not listen to what Thomas said. He made Thomas do as he was told.

In 1162 Thomas became Archbishop of Canterbury (the head of the Church of England). It was a disaster.

The quarrel, 1164–70

Henry made a law saying that the king's law courts were more important than the Church law courts. But Thomas did not agree to this. So Henry sent Thomas to live in France.

They did not speak to each other for six years.

Thomas comes back

Thomas came back to Canterbury in 1170. But as soon as Thomas came back, he and Henry quarrelled again.

Henry lost his temper

This time Henry really lost his temper. Four knights heard him shouting. They wanted to please the king, so they decided to murder Thomas Becket.

Source B

An eyewitness describes the murder of Thomas Becket.

On 29 December 1170, the four knights rode into Canterbury. They found Thomas and told him to leave the country. Thomas refused. There were some monks with him. They rushed Thomas into the cathedral. They thought he would be safe there. But the knights followed. They struck Thomas down in front of the altar. They sliced through his skull and his blood and brains splattered over the floor of the cathedral.

Questions

1 Read **Henry II wanted control**.
   Write down the three things Henry wanted to control.

2 Read **The quarrel, 1164–70**.

   a What did Henry make a law saying?
   b Did Thomas agree with Henry's law?

3 Read Source B.
   What happened to Thomas?

What happened?

- People collected Becket's blood. They believed it would make miracles happen.

- The Pope made Thomas Becket a saint.

- Ever since 1170 pilgrims have gone to Canterbury to pray at Becket's tomb.

- The Church kept its own law courts.

- The King kept on saying who should be archbishop.

King John

Henry II's younger son, John, became king in 1199. He did not keep control. Under King John, the barons were very strong. Barons were noblemen who paid for the king's army through their taxes.

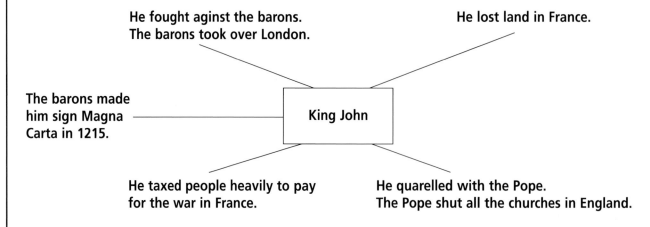

He fought aginst the barons.
The barons took over London.

He lost land in France.

The barons made him sign Magna Carta in 1215.

King John

He taxed people heavily to pay for the war in France.

He quarelled with the Pope.
The Pope shut all the churches in England.

This picture of King John signing Magna Carta was painted in the 1800s.

Source A

King John signs Magna Carta

The barons were angry with King John. They said that his taxes and laws were unfair. The barons met King John near Windsor Castle and made him sign Magna Carta. 'Magna Carta' means 'Great Charter', and it said that John must rule well.

What did the Magna Carta say?

Magna Carta was really for the barons. It did not help ordinary people much. Here are some of the things it said.

- The barons will give money for the king's army only if they want to.

- No man can be put on trial unless there are good witnesses.

- No free man can be sent to prison except by the law of the land.

- All merchants can travel safely in England.

- If you have done something wrong, you cannot pay to get out of prison.

Later King John said he had been forced to sign Magna Carta. So he said that it did not count. The barons were angry and started to fight John again.

King John died suddenly in 1216. The new king was nine years old. So the barons got their way.

ELEANOR OF AQUITAINE (1122–1204)

Eleanor was King John's mother. She was very strong willed. Even when she was over 70 years old, she led an army for her son, John.

These are the sort of clothes that Eleanor and other rich women wore.

Questions

1 Read **King John**.

   a When did John become king?
   b Who were the barons?

2 Read **What did the Magna Carta say?**
   Write down the one you think is most important for ordinary people.

A crusade or Holy War

A **crusade** was a war against people of a different religion. Christians and Muslims had different religions. They fought to control the Holy Land. The main city of the Holy Land was Jerusalem.

The First Crusade

The Muslims took over Jerusalem in 1087. The Pope was head of the Christian Church. He asked all Christians to go and take Jerusalem back.

Thousands of Christians walked, rode and set sail for Jerusalem. They were called **crusaders**.

Other crusades

There were more crusades.

They dragged on for well over 200 years.

Muslims   Jerusalem   Christians

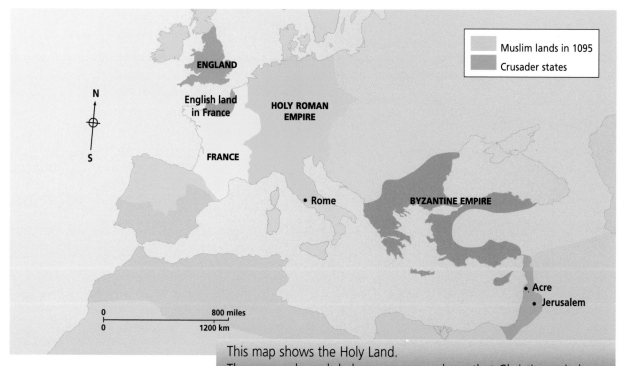

Muslim lands in 1095
Crusader states

ENGLAND

English land in France

HOLY ROMAN EMPIRE

N

S

FRANCE

• Rome

BYZANTINE EMPIRE

• Acre

• Jerusalem

0   800 miles
0   1200 km

This map shows the Holy Land.
The areas coloured dark orange were places that Christians tried to control.

Some reasons for going on a crusade.

What Saladin said

Saladin was a great Muslim leader. He did not understand why the Christians kept coming to the Holy Land to fight. He said:

- It was a long way to come.
- There were more Muslims than Christians.
- The Christians always gave up in the end and went home.

Questions

1 Read **A crusade or Holy War**.

   a What was a crusade?
   b What was the main city of the Holy Land?

2 Look at the picture above.
   Write down the main reasons why people went on crusades.

The city of Acre

The city of Acre is in the Holy Land. In 1189, during the Third Crusade, the Christians laid siege to the city. The siege went on for two years.

What was the siege like?

The Christians sat outside the city. The Muslims sat inside. Neither side gave up. The siege went on day after day. It went on month after month.

The Muslims were starving inside the city. But the Christians were starving too.

It was very hot. There was nothing to eat. The soldiers killed and ate their own horses. Sometimes they did not even skin them. They chewed bones left by dogs. They flung themselves on the ground and ate plants.

King Richard I arrives

In 1191 King Richard arrived with more soldiers. He stopped every bit of food getting to Acre.

A month later the Muslims gave up.

KING RICHARD I (1189–99)

Richard was King of England and a Christian soldier. He was brave and loved going on crusades. But he often argued with other kings and with his family.

A Muslim soldier.

A Christian soldier.

Source A

This picture of the siege of Acre was painted in 1280.

The soldiers are wearing armour. But many soldiers threw their armour away. It was too hot and too heavy to wear.

This picture, painted in about 1280, shows women attacking their enemies.

Women crusaders

The King said women must not go on crusades. But some women did. They went to fight, or to look after the soldiers.

Some of them were wives. Some women joined the crusade when it got to the Holy Land.

Washerwomen

Women who washed clothes for a living were allowed to go on crusades. So there were washerwomen at the siege of Acre.

Acre was near the sea. So they probably did the washing in sea water.

Catching the washerwomen

The washerwomen were very fierce. If the Muslims caught any washerwomen by mistake, they sent them straight back to the crusaders.

ONE WOMAN

Some women were carrying earth to fill the ditch round the city. One woman was cut down by a Muslim spear. Her husband ran to her. She asked him to use her dead body to fill the ditch.

Question

Read the box **Richard I (1189-99)**.
Write down one sentence about Richard.

Things people brought back from the crusades

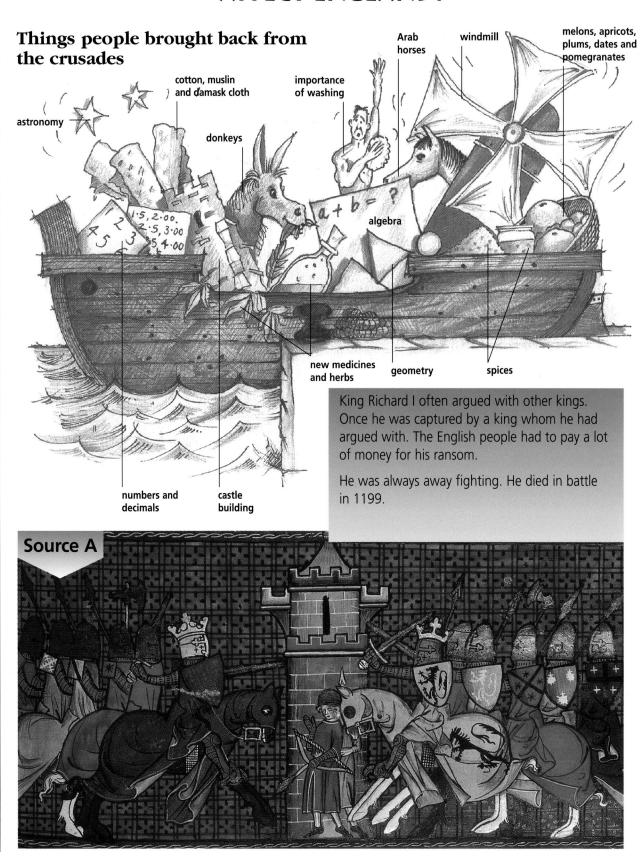

astronomy

cotton, muslin and damask cloth

importance of washing

Arab horses

windmill

melons, apricots, plums, dates and pomegranates

donkeys

$a + b = ?$

algebra

new medicines and herbs

geometry

spices

numbers and decimals

castle building

King Richard I often argued with other kings. Once he was captured by a king whom he had argued with. The English people had to pay a lot of money for his ransom.

He was always away fighting. He died in battle in 1199.

Source A

Learning from the Muslims

The crusaders did not fight with the Muslims all the time. When they were not fighting, the crusaders learnt a lot from the Muslims.

They learnt better ways of building. They learnt the importance of fresh food and regular baths. They learnt how to use Arabic numbers (the numbers we use today).

They also learnt lots of important things about medicine. A Muslim doctor described a visit to a Christian camp in about 1150:

They took me to see a knight with a boil on his leg. I put a **poultice** *on the leg, and it began to heal.*

Then a French doctor came. He sent for a man with an axe. He said to the man 'strike hard and cleanly'. The marrow spurted out of the bone when it was cut. The knight died at once.

How did the Third Crusade affect England?

- Many people died.

- The King was always away fighting.

- The King taxed ordinary people to pay for the crusade.

- The King left his brother John to run the country.

Source B

Muslim doctors were more respected by their patients than European doctors were.

They knew more about drugs and keeping clean.

Question

Look at **Things people brought back from the crusades**.
Write down six of them.

Who owned the village?

The king

I own all the land in England.

I let my Norman lords farm the land.

In return they must fight for me and bring soldiers when I need them.

The lord and the villagers

The lord was given the village land by the king. The villagers worked on the lord's land. They could keep some of the crops they grew.

If there was a war, the villagers had to go with their lord. They had to fight for the king.

The lord

The lord was the most important person in the village.

Lord and lady of the manor, 1250.

The miller was important. The villagers paid him to grind their wheat and barley into flour.

Source A

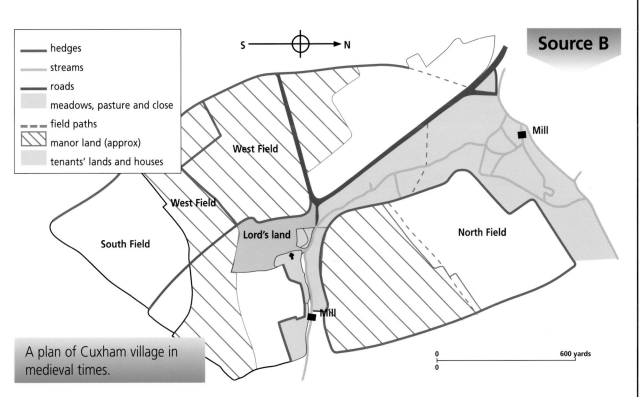

Key:
- hedges
- streams
- roads
- meadows, pasture and close
- field paths
- manor land (approx)
- tenants' lands and houses

S ← → N

West Field

West Field

South Field

Lord's land

North Field

Mill

Mill

0
0   600 yards

A plan of Cuxham village in medieval times.

Farming the land

There were three big fields. Each year:

- One field grew wheat.
- One field grew barley, oats and rye.
- One field was left to rest.

Each field was divided into strips.

This is a typical field divided into strips:

Lord's strip
Lord's strip
Lord's strip
Lord's strip
Villager A's strip
Villager B's strip
Priest's strip
Villager C's strip
Villager D's strip
Priest's strip
Villager E's strip
Villager F's strip
Villager E's strip

ALL GROWING WHEAT

The priest

The priest ran the church in the village.

He baptised, married and buried the villagers.

Questions

Read the boxes **The lord** and **The priest**.

a Who was the most important person in the village?

b What did the priest do?

45

Cuxham is a village in Oxfordshire.

In medieval times, the lord and the priest were the most important people in the village. But what were the other villagers like?

ROBERT OLDMAN – THE REEVE

Robert Oldman was the **reeve** at Cuxham. One of his jobs was buying and selling crops and animals for the lord.

Robert brewed most of the beer in the village.

In 1313 he went to a place called Abingdon. He bought an ox there and set off home. But he stayed the night at an inn. The ox got away and in the morning it was nowhere to be seen. It took Robert two days to find the ox.

Robert must have been good at his job. He worked as reeve from 1311 until his death in 1349.

The reeve's job

- He made sure everyone did their jobs.
- At harvest time he used extra people to work in the fields.
- He sold spare crops and animals.

Questions

1 Read **The reeve's job**. Write down the 3 things the reeve did.

2 Read **Joan Overchurch**. Write down the two ways that the lord helped Joan when her house was burned down.

Source A

Most village women kept hens.

The village shepherd looked after the sheep.

JOAN OVERCHURCH

Joan Overchurch was married to John. They were comfortably off. They paid rent to the lord instead of working.

But John died in 1311. Soon after, Joan's house burnt down. The lord said she did not have to pay rent for her land for a year.

The lord also gave her some wheat and barley to help her.

Joan passed all her land over to her son Elias. She moved into a small cottage.

JOHN GREEN

John Green was well off. He rented land in Cuxham and other villages too. In 1315 he owned an ox. The only other people who owned an ox in the village were the lord and the priest.

John and his wife, Matilda, had three sons. They were called John, Thomas and Hugh.

Harvest time was one of the busiest times of the year. The whole village was out in the fields working. These pictures of harvest time were drawn in the 1300s.

In the picture below, the workers are cutting wheat and making it into bundles.

In the picture on page 46 a horse and cart is taking the bundles away.

The fishpond

This was used to keep fish in for the lord of the manor. Sometimes the fish got so big that they ate ducklings that were on the pond!

Who worked on the lord's land?

Full time:

- 4 ploughmen
- 1 carter
- 1 cowman and 1 helper
- 1 shepherd
- 1 gardener

Part time

- 1 woman to change barley into malt (for beer)
- 1 pig keeper
- 1 blacksmith
- Extra men and women at harvest time
- Builders and thatchers (roof makers)

The barns

The barns were used to store:

wheat barley hay straw oats peas and beans.

The lord's house

This house was made of stone.

The living rooms were on the first floor.

The lavatory was built over the stream.

What happened to the crops?

Wheat
* Some sold, some for seed, some for wages, some for the lord

Barley and oats
* Some sold, some barley for beer, some oats to feed animals

Apples
* Sold as fruit or cider

Vegetables
* Eaten by lord and servants

Questions

1 Look at the picture.

   a What was the fishpond for?

   b What were the barns for?

2 Read **What happened to the crops?**
   What happened to the wheat?

What did people do all day?

Got up at sunrise.
Worked in the fields.

Midday meal in the fields –
beer, bread and cheese.

Worked all afternoon.

Supper and to bed
at nightfall.

Special jobs

Some people had special jobs. They worked as shepherds, pig keepers, cowmen, thatchers, blacksmiths or carpenters.

Food

To eat
Bread was eaten all year round. So was cheese and bacon. But some food was difficult to store. Cherries were eaten only in the summer.

To drink
Most families made their own beer. It was more watery than beer is today.

Some villagers at work. They are weeding thistles from a field, carding wool (brushing the wool to straighten it) and spinning the wool.

Source A

Time off

The villagers worked from sunrise to sunset. But they had Sunday off.

Sundays and holy days

On Sundays and holy days, the villagers had to go to church. But they did have some time to themselves. Most villagers had about 15 holy days a year. This is where the word 'holiday' comes from.

Easter

One of the great holy days was Easter. The Church celebrated Jesus Christ. Everybody celebrated the spring. Winter was hard and there was not much food. Now, at Easter, the hens started laying eggs again. The cows were giving milk. There was a feast for everyone.

Babies and children

Babies were wrapped tightly in cloth strips. This made them sleep a lot.

Their mothers took them to work. They hung them on a hook or a branch.

Children had jobs. They picked stones off the fields or they scared birds from the seed.

As they got older, they were given harder jobs.

Jobs in the year

Spring:
- Plough.
- Sow seed.
- Shear sheep.
- Put animals outdoors.

Summer:
- Harvest.
- Pick fruit.

Autumn:
- Thresh.
- Plough.
- Sow winter wheat.
- Store hay.
- Kill pigs.
- Put meat in salt.

Winter:
- Mend tools.
- Mend fences.
- Put animals in barns.

All year:
- Work in garden.
- Brew beer, make cheese, spin wool.

Questions

1 Look at the box **Food**.

    a Write down the 2 sorts of fruit shown.

    b Write down any other fruit you eat. Do you know what country each comes from?

2 Read **Jobs in the year**. What time do you think was the busiest?

The manor court

Each village had a court. It was called the manor court and was often held in the church.

The manor courts kept records. We can read about village crimes in these records. Some crimes in the village of Cuxham are listed in the box.

What we know

We know about small crimes like stealing rabbits or not working on the lord's land.

What we don't know

We don't know about crimes like murder. The king's courts dealt with murder.

You have to look at different records to find out about these crimes.

Cuxham crimes

John Green
1320 Fined for grazing his sheep on the lord's land.

Robert Oldman
1333 Fined in the manor court for grazing his animals on the lord's land.

John Oldman
1340 Fined for stealing wood from the lord's land.

Ellis Miller
1374 Arrested for serious stealing. He was sentenced to death. But he escaped and was never seen again.

The boy is stealing cherries.

The owner of the tree looks as if he is going to beat the boy.

A lot of small crime was punished this way.

Source A

THE PILLORY

THE STOCKS

What about the towns?

Towns had more crime than villages. This is not surprising. There were more people and more things to steal.

Most people who stole did it because they were poor.

Punishment

There were no prisons in early medieval times. Important people could be locked up in Royal castles.

Other people were punished by being put in the stocks or the pillory.

Or they had to pay fines of money.

Sometimes they were put to death for serious crimes.

Distraint:— Taking goods to pay a fine...

TUG PULL

FINES

Some of the punishments given out for minor crimes.

Questions

Read **Punishment**.

a Write down the 3 sorts of punishment.

b Which one was for serious crime?

c What happens to people today who commit serious crimes.

The English king's job

The English king had two jobs:

1 To keep England safe.

2 To make England bigger.

How to do the job

1 Keeping England safe meant controlling Wales, Scotland and Ireland.

2 Making England bigger meant taking land in Wales, Scotland and Ireland.

Swearing fealty

The English kings wanted the kings of Wales, Scotland and Ireland to swear to obey the king of England.

Source A

The King of Scotland is swearing to obey the King of England in 1296. This is what England wanted.

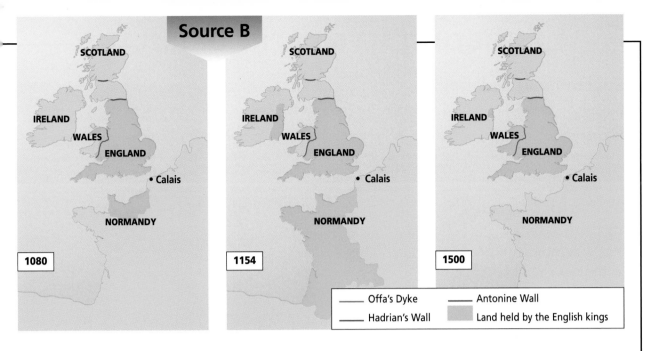

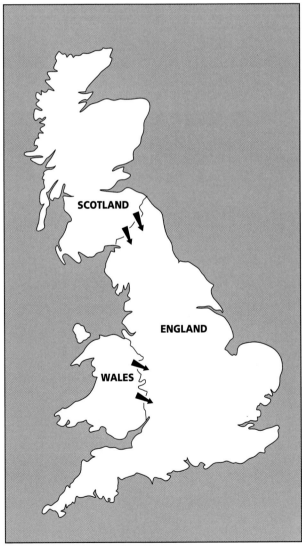

Source B

| Offa's Dyke | Antonine Wall |
| Hadrian's Wall | Land held by the English kings |

1080 · 1154 · 1500

Land held by English kings in 1080, 1154 and 1500. All the kings of the four countries took as much land as they could.

The four countries – England, Scotland, Wales, and Ireland

The four countries helped each other when it suited them.

The Scots and Welsh often invaded England.

Questions

1 Read **The English king's job**.
   Write down the two jobs the English king had.

2 Read **How to do the job**.
   How did the English king keep England safe?

England and Ireland

England wanted to control Ireland. But Ireland was hard to control.

- It was separated from England by sea.
- It was big and split into lots of kingdoms.

Irish kings fighting

The Irish kings fought each other. One of the kings was **Dermot McMurrough**. He was king of a place in Ireland called Leinster.

But after he lost a big battle in 1152, Dermot McMurrough fled to England.

Henry II and Dermot

King Henry II of England said he would help Dermot. There were two sides to this:

1 Dermot swore **fealty** to Henry.
This meant Dermot would be loyal to Henry.

2 Henry said he would help Dermot against the other Irish kings.

The English lords who went to Ireland often became Irish themselves:

Many of them have given up their own language (English). Instead they use the language and the ways of life of the Irish.

Henry II
English king

Dermot
King of Leinster

Other Irish kings

Henry saw himself as top king.

Source A

An Irish carving from medieval times. The Irish lords have long hair and beards. The Normans said this made the Irish look wild.

DERMOT AND STRONGBOW

Who was Dermot McMurrough?

He was a big, fierce man. In 1131 he was 20 years old. He had an argument with the Abbess of a nunnery. People said he won the argument. He kidnapped the Abbess, killed all the nuns and burned the Abbey to the ground.

Strongbow was an English lord. He went to Ireland and fought for Dermot McMurrough. They won. Strongbow married Dermot's daughter.

Always fighting

Dermot fought all the other kings and lords. He kidnapped one lord's wife and burned all his castles down. In the end Dermot himself was driven out of Ireland. He fled across the sea and met Henry II.

Back in Ireland

Dermot got back his land with Henry's help. He was as fierce and warlike as ever. Some other Irish kings captured Dermot's son and said they would kill him if Dermot did not stop. Dermot said go ahead and kill him – so they did. Dermot died in 1171.

Death of Dermot

When Dermot died in 1171, Strongbow became King of Leinster.

Source B

A painting from about 1200 of a Norman knight in Ireland. He has English armour, but has grown long hair and a beard, like the Irish.

Henry II and Strongbow

Henry was worried. Strongbow was too powerful. Maybe he would attack England. But Strongbow did not want to fight. In the end, Strongbow and Henry met.

1 Strongbow swore fealty to Henry.

2 Henry said he would help Strongbow against the other Irish kings.

Henry as top king

Henry did not go to Ireland with Dermot. But later he went to Ireland with Strongbow.

Several Irish kings swore to be loyal to Henry. This meant that Henry was top king.

Question

Read **England and Ireland**.
Why was Ireland hard to control?
Give two reasons.

William and Wales in 1066

William of Normandy was busy ruling England. So he gave land in Wales to his Norman friends. They gradually took over a lot of South Wales.

Edward I and Wales in 1272

Edward I was a strong king. He wanted to rule all of Wales.

South Wales was easy to control because it was flat and easy to fight in. But North Wales was full of mountains.

Llewelyn and North Wales

Part of North Wales was ruled by **Llewelyn ap Gryffyd**. When Edward I attacked in 1277, Llewelyn led his people into the mountains.

At first, the English could not get at them. But in the end the Welsh had to give themselves up to the English.

Llewelyn and his brother were killed. Edward I had won.

Source A

The Chronicle of Lanercost was written at the time. It describes the punishment of Llewelyn's brother, David:

David had his insides cut out of his stomach for being a traitor. He was then hung for being a thief. His arms and legs were cut off for being a rebel.

Source B

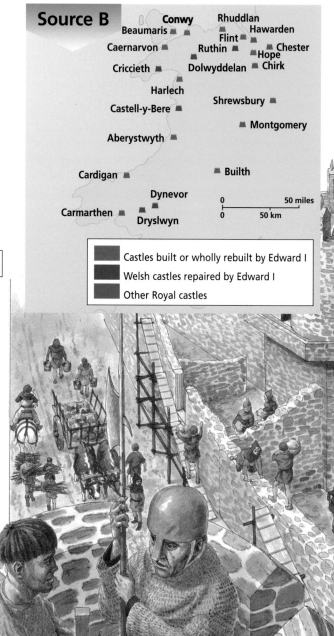

Conwy, Rhuddlan, Beaumaris, Hawarden, Caernarvon, Flint, Chester, Hope, Ruthin, Criccieth, Dolwyddelan, Chirk, Harlech, Shrewsbury, Castell-y-Bere, Montgomery, Aberystwyth, Cardigan, Builth, Dynevor, Carmarthen, Dryslwyn

Castles built or wholly rebuilt by Edward I
Welsh castles repaired by Edward I
Other Royal castles

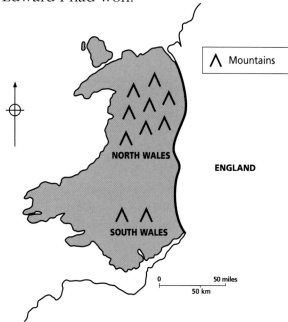

Mountains

NORTH WALES

ENGLAND

SOUTH WALES

0   50 miles
   50 km

The English took over South Wales. But it was difficult to take North Wales. There were so many mountains.

What did Edward I do to keep the Welsh down?

- Edward built eight new castles.
- He built Conwy Castle in the most important town.
- He built a new town around the castle.
- He made his own son Prince of Wales.

Conwy Castle

Conwy Castle was started in 1283. It took four years to build.

The castle cost £20,000 to build (£2 million in today's money).

Men came from all over Britain to build the castle. They worked from the beginning of February to the end of October. They worked from sunrise to sunset. They worked six days a week. It was a magnificent castle. Edward built it to make sure that the Welsh knew the English were staying.

Well designed

The castle was so well built it took only 30 men to defend it and look after it.

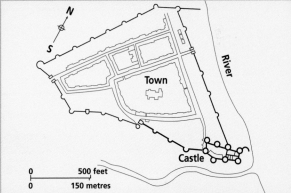

Source C

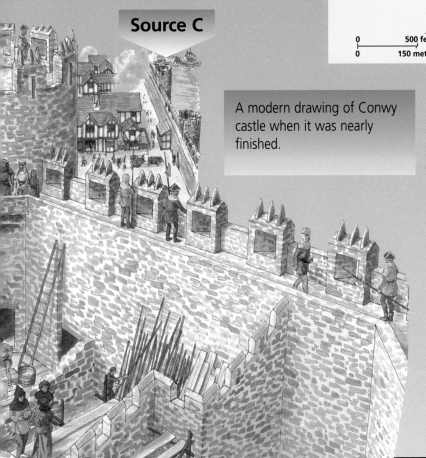

A modern drawing of Conwy castle when it was nearly finished.

Questions

1 Read **What did Edward I do to keep the Welsh down?** How many castles did Edward build?

2 Read **Conwy Castle**.

   a How much did Conwy Castle cost to build?

   b How much is that worth today?

3 Read **Well designed**. How many men looked after or defended Conwy Castle?

William and Scotland

William of Normandy was busy ruling England. But some of his Norman friends went to live in Scotland.

The years went by. The Normans married into Scottish families and became Scots. They did not want to be ruled by the King of England.

Edward I

Edward I did not like this. He wanted to rule all of England, Wales and Scotland. He had conquered Wales. Now he wanted Scotland.

Edward conquers Scotland

Edward marched to Scotland. By 1305 he had defeated the Scots. He killed their leader, **William Wallace**.

Had Edward won?

Edward had won. But would it last?

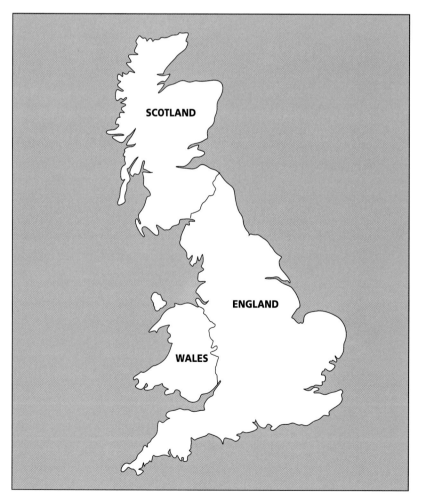

Swearing fealty

Edward I forced the Scottish king to swear fealty (loyalty) to him. He seized the Scottish Crown Jewels and the Stone of Scone too. The Stone of Scone is the seat on which Scottish kings were crowned.

Source A

Edward I wanted the Scottish kings to swear fealty to him. But this is what one Scottish king said:

No one has the right to ask me to swear fealty for my kingdom. To God alone will I do this.

Source B

King David II of Scotland with King Edward III of England. They are shaking hands as equals. Compare this to Source A on page 54.

ROBERT BRUCE

Robert Bruce was crowned King of Scotland in 1306. Edward I was furious.

Edward marched to Scotland and killed Bruce's family or put them in prison. But Bruce got away.

Bruce in hiding

Bruce had a few friends. They hid all through the long, cold winter. Sometimes they lived in caves.

The story of Bruce and the spider

Bruce nearly gave up. But one day he saw a spider. It tried over and over again to make its web. Finally it made the web.

This made Bruce think he must go on trying.

Victory at last

Edward I died in 1307. This was Bruce's lucky break. Edward II was a weak king.

Bruce beat the English at the Battle of Bannockburn in 1314. Some years later, Edward III agreed that Scotland should have its own king.

Source C

Robert Bruce, painted in 1306

Questions

1 Read **Edward I**.
   What did Edward want?

2 Read **Edward conquers Scotland**.
   By what date had Edward defeated the Scots?

3 Read **Robert Bruce**.

   a When did Robert Bruce beat the English?
   b What was the name of the battle?

The population of Britain was growing

The population of Britain was growing in medieval times. More and more people lived in villages and towns. More people needed more food.

Why did towns get bigger?

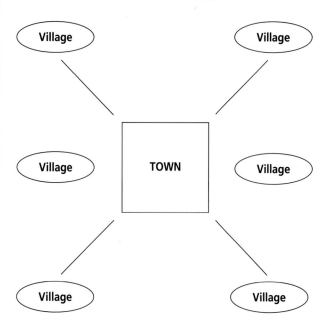

- Villagers grew more food.
- They sold it in the town.
- More people went to live in the town.
- They sold things to the villagers to take home.

London in 1066

London was the biggest town in England. It was a jumble of houses, people, shops and animals.

It was very dirty. People threw rubbish into the streets. They threw rubbish into the rivers. But people also got their water from the rivers and springs.

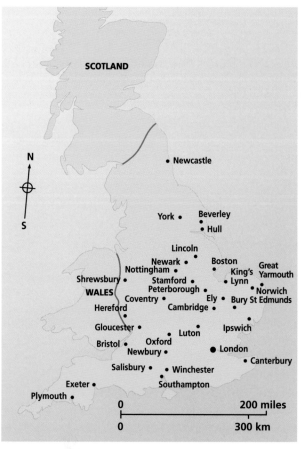

The main towns in England in the 1400s.

London in 1200

London got much bigger. By 1200 the River Thames was filthy. So were the springs and wells nearby. Most people drank beer because it was safer.

Clean water for London

From 1237 people built pipes. These pipes carried clean water from the country. The pipes were made from hollowed-out trees or lead.

Source A

This drawing of London Bridge was made around 1500.
The houses were crowded.
The lavatories emptied into the River Thames.

Source B

Part of a letter written in 1349 from King Edward III to the Lord Mayor of London.

This is an order to take away the filth in the streets.

The king has learnt that the city is foul with filth. The air is infected, so people are in danger.

Rich men's houses were made of brick or stone.

Some houses were thatched. Rats and fleas lived in the thatch.

London houses in medieval times.

Poor men's houses were made of mud, sticks and horse-hair.

Medieval and modern London.

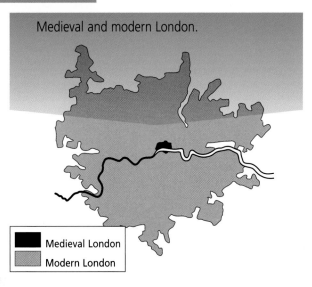

■ Medieval London
▨ Modern London

Questions

1 Look at the drawing of London street houses. What lived in the thatch?

2 Look at Source B.

   a Where did the filth go?
   b Why does the King think people are in danger?

Town charters

Many towns grew. They wanted to make their own rules. Below is a list of the sort of things towns needed to have rules about:

- when to shut the town gates
- running markets
- collecting tax money
- having law courts
- street cleaning
- building houses.

But towns needed a **charter** from the king before they could make their own rules.

The town charter of Lincoln

The king gave Lincoln a charter in 1129. Then the people of Lincoln chose a **mayor** and other men to run the town.

These men ran everything from the law courts to the town crier, who let everyone know the town news.

What made Lincoln a rich town?

English wool was the best in Europe. Some of the best wool came from around Lincoln. So there was lots of work for people in Lincoln. The best wool went across the sea to Flanders. They wove very fine wool cloth.

English cloth

The English made rougher, thicker wool cloth. The cloth was used to make clothes for soldiers and working people.

Source A

There were eleven markets in Lincoln. Everyone who sold things at the market had to pay taxes.

On every horse	1d
On every cow	½d
On 24 young sheep	1d
On a big bag of corn	2d

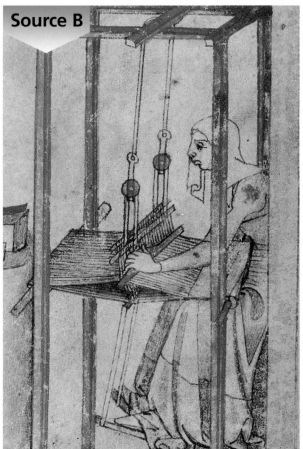

Source B

This picture of a woman weaving cloth was drawn sometime between 1350 and 1375.

Guilds – workers get together

A **guild** was a group of people who worked in the same trade. Here are some guilds:

- shoemakers
- goldsmiths
- butchers
- cloth makers.

In Lincoln there were eleven guilds.

Learning a trade

Apprentice

learns from **master**
for several years

becomes a

Journeyman

then later becomes a

Master

and then teaches
apprentices.

Source C

The people who ran Lincoln decided the prices of things sold at the market. Here are some prices from 1361:

10 eggs	**1d**
3 roast thrushes	**2d**
1 roast pig	**8d**

Source D

This painting, made in 1482, shows a guild master judging the work of men who want to become masters. He will decide whether or not they are good enough.

Questions

1 Read **Town charters**.

  a Write down two things that a town needed to have rules about.

  b Who gave a charter to the town?

  c Which rule would not work in a town today?

2 Read **Guilds – workers get together**. What was a guild?

What is a merchant?

A **merchant** buys from one person and sells to another.

Merchants had ships to bring rolls of cloth to England. They brought spices and furs too. Most merchants were men. But sometimes a merchant died and his wife ran his business.

Abingdon	Soap Clay Iron	**Reading**	Tin
Alton	Wine Dye Clay Resin Salt	**Romsey**	Wine Fish Garlic Silk Coal Iron Dye
Andover	Onions Soap Wax Iron Fish		
Bristol	Dye Soap Wine	**Salisbury**	Wine Fish Dye Flax Soap Canvas Dried fruits Timber Building materials Household furnishings
Exeter	Dye		
Gloucester	Dye Soap Oil		
Honiton	Dye	**Wilton**	Dye Oil Wine Flax
Leicester	Dye	**Winchester**	Fish Wine Oil Salt Garlic Iron Soap Dye
Oxford	Wine Dye Millstones		

Source A

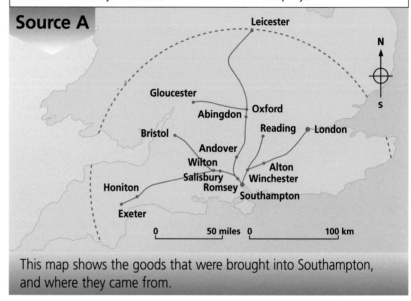

This map shows the goods that were brought into Southampton, and where they came from.

Source B

A picture of a medieval street with shops, painted in about 1460.

A packhorse train.

DAME CLARAMUNDA – A MEDIEVAL BUSINESSWOMAN

Dame Claramunda was married twice. When her husbands died, she ran their businesses.

She was such a good merchant that Henry III asked her to buy all his wine in France in 1258.

This is the way she might have dressed.

Southampton and trade

Southampton was a port. So merchants had ships. They sailed to Europe and brought back wine and silk. They loaded the wine and silk on **packhorses**. Then they sold them all over England.

Source C

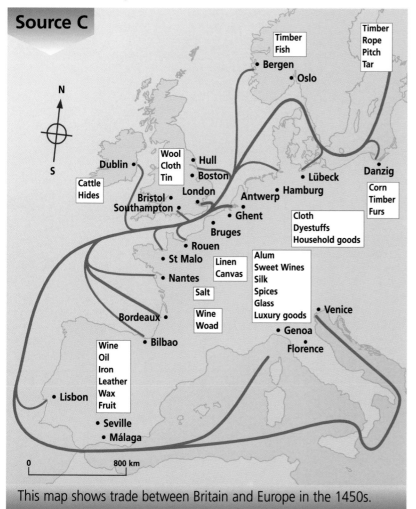

Timber
Fish
• Bergen
• Oslo

Timber
Rope
Pitch
Tar

N

S

Dublin •

Wool
Cloth
Tin

• Hull
• Boston

• Lübeck

Danzig

Cattle
Hides

Bristol •
Southampton •

London

Antwerp •

Hamburg

Corn
Timber
Furs

• Ghent

Cloth
Dyestuffs
Household goods

• Bruges

• Rouen

• St Malo

Linen
Canvas

Alum
Sweet Wines
Silk
Spices
Glass
Luxury goods

• Venice

• Nantes

Salt

Bordeaux •

Wine
Woad

• Genoa
Florence

• Bilbao

Wine
Oil
Iron
Leather
Wax
Fruit

• Lisbon

• Seville
• Málaga

0   800 km

This map shows trade between Britain and Europe in the 1450s.

Questions

1 What does a merchant do?

2 Look at Source A.

   a What did merchants buy in Bristol?
   b What did they buy in Winchester?
   c What did they buy in Reading?
   d What did they buy in Exeter?

3 Read **Dame Claramunda.**

   a What did Dame Claramunda do when her husbands died?
   b Why did Henry III ask her to buy his wine?

Bells not clocks

When the sun came up, the bell ringer rang the town bell. The town gates were opened up. At night the bell ringer rang the bell. The gates were closed.

Baths and lavatories

People went to public bath-houses. They used outside lavatories, or poured their waste into the street.

You can see the channel in the street for the waste to run down.

Street cries

Lots of women, men and children sold things on the street. Here are some of the things they sold:

hot apple pies   hot mutton pies hot oatcakes   fresh herrings   cherries apples   rabbits.

They shouted out what they were selling.

A well-off person's house in medieval times. This is a modern painting.

Getting ill

Doctors charged a lot of money. So the women who looked after their families often made their own medicine:

feverfew for fevers and headaches

sage tea for a sore throat

nettle tea for aching bones.

Source A

Cooking

Some houses did not have a kitchen. So women took uncooked bread to a baker. He cooked it in his oven.

Sometimes women or servants took food such as fruit to a pie-maker so he could make the pastry and cook the pie.

Question

Look at the picture.
Find the following:

The fire

The water stored in the house

The windows

The cradle

The broom

The man carrying water

The woman pouring waste onto the street.

The channel carrying rubbish and waste away.

Kitchens

Kitchens were often built in the yard. This was because the kitchen might catch fire.

Most kitchens had bunches of twigs for whisking eggs and cream. There were pots and pans, knives and things for grinding herbs and spices.

What was the Black Death?

The Black Death started in 1346. It was a terrible disease.

Most people died in a few days. It killed millions of people and animals.

Where did it start?

The Black Death started in the East. Then it spread all over Europe.

Sailors caught the Black Death and then they sailed home. The Black Death came with them.

The Black Death moved quickly through towns. People in towns lived very close together. There were also more rats and other animals in towns to pass on the disease.

How the Black Death spread

The Black Death was carried by fleas which lived on rats. These fleas gave people and animals the Black Death by biting them.

Source A

Burying people who died of the Black Death.

Source B

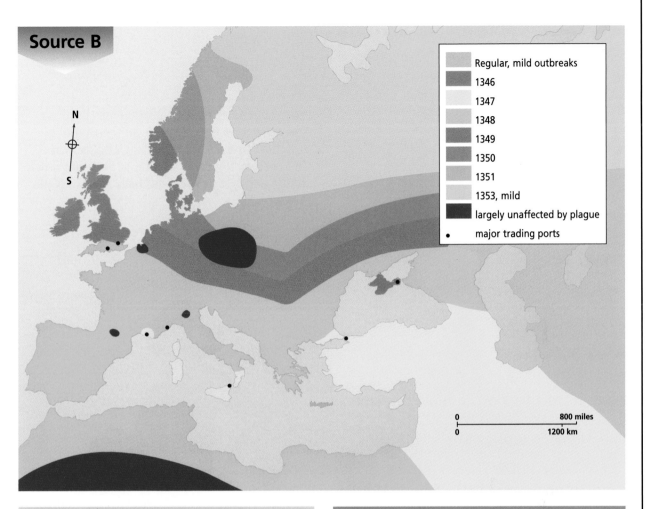

Legend:
- Regular, mild outbreaks
- 1346
- 1347
- 1348
- 1349
- 1350
- 1351
- 1353, mild
- largely unaffected by plague
- • major trading ports

0 — 800 miles
0 — 1200 km

How the Black Death spread, 1346–53.

Source C

A writer in Italy said that God sent the Black Death to punish people.

God sent the Black Death in the East first. Then it spread through the world.

This terrible sickness was carried by sick people from the East.

By sight, or touch, or breathing on others, they killed everyone.

Signs of the Black Death

- Big swellings in the armpit and groin.
- The swellings turned black.
- Most people died.

Questions

1 Look at the box **How the Black Death spread**.

   a What animals gave people the Black Death?

   b How did these animals give the Black Death to people?

What to do about the Black Death

There were three things a person could do if they had the Black Death.

1 Get ready to die

Many people believed that God had sent the Black Death. So there was no point trying to cure it.

All you could do was say sorry to God for doing bad things. Then you would go to Heaven.

2 Run away

Many people ran away from London and other towns. Sometimes they took the illness with them.

3 See a doctor

Doctors did not know what caused the Black Death. Some took blood from the patient, or gave them herbs. Others charged huge sums of money for cures that did not work.

Trying to control the Black Death

The people who ran some of the towns tried to control the Black Death. They tried to keep sick people away from the others, and to bury dead bodies quickly.

Dying properly

Some people thought that to get to Heaven you had to die properly. This meant seeing a priest before you died and then having a proper burial.

But many people did not have these things. This made their families very upset.

Source A

This is what a writer in Italy said about the Black Death.

Wives ran away from their husbands. Brothers ran away from each other. Even the clothes of a victim could kill. One death in a house was followed by the death of all the rest, right down to the dogs. Doctors did not have a cure for the Black Death.

Source B

The doctor is taking blood from a patient.

Some doctors thought that too much blood made you ill.

Questions

Look at the picture above.

a Write down one idea that people had about what caused the Black Death.

b Why would keeping the streets clear of rubbish help to stop the Black Death?

Many died

The Black Death killed more than half the adults in Cuxham village.

New people came

New people came to live in Cuxham. But often they did not stay long.

It was difficult for the lord to find a man to be the reeve and run the village.

Money

The new villagers did not want to have to work on the lord's land. So the lord and the new villagers made an agreement.

You pay me for your cottage and land.

You pay us for working for you.

Burning the clothes of people who had died of the Black Death.

Source A

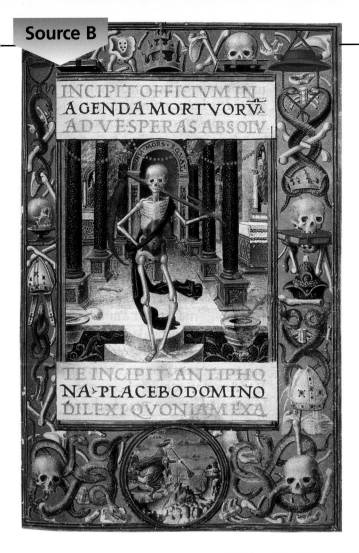

After the Black Death, pictures of Death appeared all over Europe.

Questions

Read **Robert Oldman and his family**.

a When did Robert die?
b What do you think happened to Richard and Robert?

PEOPLE IN CUXHAM

JOHN GREEN AND HIS FAMILY

John Green and his son John survived the Black Death. But another son, Thomas, died.

After the Black Death, the two Johns mainly kept sheep. One man could look after a lot of sheep. Maybe there were not enough men to plough and dig and grow crops.

ROBERT OLDMAN AND HIS FAMILY

Robert died in March 1349.

Then his wife died.

Then his son John died.

We do not know what happened to the other sons, Richard and and Robert. They are not heard of again in the lord's records.

JOAN OVERCHURCH

Joan was dead before the Black Death. But her son Elias and his family died.

HENRY GARDENER

Henry Gardener survived the Black Death. He even became better off because so many other people died.

9.4 HOW DID THE BLACK DEATH AFFECT OTHER PLACES?

We have seen how the Black Death affected people in Cuxham. But what was it like in other places?

Many parts of France

About one in ten lived.

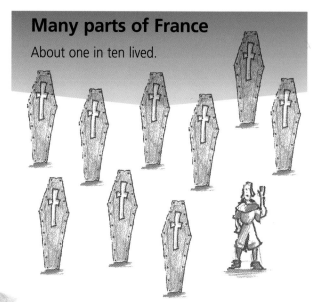

Genoa, Italy

One in seven lived.

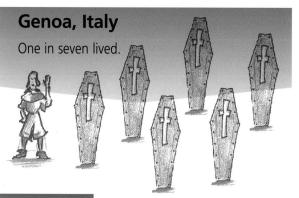

Source A

Before the Black Death... **After the Black Death..**

Lots of people...

Lots of workers need land, so...

the lord...

need food...

Fewer workers...

lots of land...

Fewer people...

need less food..

asks for a lot of work, not rent...

workers ask a lot for their work...

so food prices go down...

pay rent, work less...

move about more...

and doesn't let his workers move about.

will do extra work but only for pay!

and animals are kept more and need fewer workers.

After the Black Death there were fewer people so workers asked for a lot of money for their work.

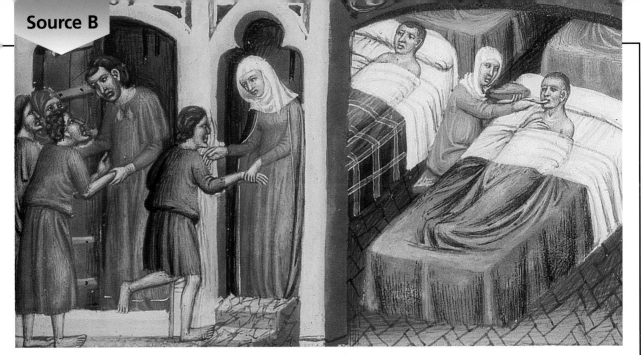

Source B

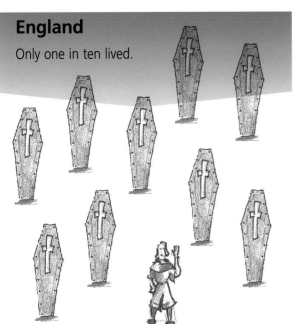

England

Only one in ten lived.

Many monks looked after the sick people with the Black Death. Many of the monks died.

Source C

This is what the King of England said in 1349:

Many farm workers have died. The farm workers who are left want more money. This makes farming difficult.

So we order that any man or woman under the age of 60 must work. They must work for the same money as they got before the Black Death.

Questions

Look at Source A. Read **After the Black Death**. Fill in the gaps in these sentences using the word box opposite.

a After the Black Death, there were _____ workers.

b After the Black Death, the workers asked for _____ money.

c After the Black Death, the price of food went _____.

a lot of	down	fewer

The Black Death

The Black Death killed thousands of people. Who would plant the crops? Who would look after the chickens, sheep and cows?

Higher wages

The lords who held the land were desperate. There were only a few labourers left. So the lords offered labourers more money.

**Here is more money.
Please work on my land.**

John Ball

John Ball was a priest. He said that all people were created equal by God. What he said frightened rich people. But poor labourers listened to him and agreed.

The Poll Tax

Poll is another word for head. So the Poll Tax was a tax on heads.

4 heads = 4 people to pay Poll Tax.

The king and the lords

The king and the lords did not like the labourers getting more money. So they decided to pass a law in Parliament.

The Statute of Labourers, 1351

This new law was called the Statute of Labourers. It said that labourers must only be paid the same money as before the Black Death.

This made the labourers angry.

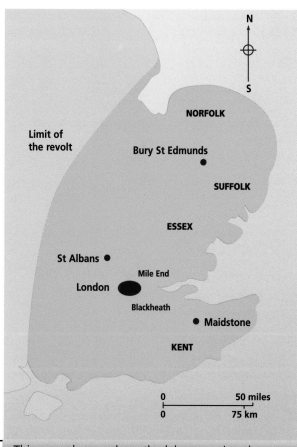

This map shows where the labourers rioted.

Source A

This poem was written at the time of the Peasants' Revolt:

When Adam dug and Eve span, who was then a gentleman?

Source B

John Ball leading a group of peasants. The picture was painted in 1460.

Why did the king set the Poll Tax?

The king needed money to fight France. He taxed everyone over the age of 15 years. This was called the Poll Tax.

What people had to pay

1377   4d per person
1379   4d per person
1381   12d per person
This was a lot of money for a poor person to pay.

What happened?

Labourers in Essex rioted. Labourers in Kent rioted too. They were led by Wat Tyler. They marched on London.

The Peasants' Revolt had begun. Peasant is another word for a poor labourer.

Source C

From the Statute of Labourers.

Men shall work for the same money they were paid before the Black Death or they will be put in prison.

Questions

Read **The Statute of Labourers, 1351**.

a What did the Statute of Labourers say?
b How did the labourers feel about this?

Where did the rebels come from?

The peasants who rebelled came from different places. They came from Essex, Kent, Suffolk and Norfolk.

Who were they?

Many of the people who rebelled were poor labourers – but not all.

Peasant rebels in Suffolk

The court records of Suffolk tell us about some of these people.

WILLIAM METEFIELD

William was first in court in 1369. It was said he 'drew blood' from Alice Godhave.

In 1377 he was fined for brewing too much ale.

In 1381 William led a band of peasants in Norfolk. They robbed and looted.

He is never heard of again.

MARGARET WRIGHTE

We know about very few women in the Peasants' Revolt.

Margaret was in court in 1379. She was fined for brewing too much ale.

In 1381 she was accused of killing a judge. But we do not know what happened to her.

JOHN HARAS

We first hear of John when he was on a jury in 1371.

In 1381 he joined a group of peasants attacking a manor.

He was pardoned in 1383.

N

S

● Brandon
● Lakenheath

● Herringswell

■ BURY ST EDMUNDS

SUFFOLK

● Kersey   ● Aldham   ■ IPS

Fe

0
0

25 miles
25 km

ADAM ROGGE

In 1360 Adam was in court for arguing with his mother.

In 1361 he was in court for beating up Thomas Elenesfenne.

In 1371 he was in court over money, then later for letting cows get out.

In 1381 Adam was looking after his lord's land. But on 14 June 1381 he joined the peasant rebels.

They attacked houses and stole money.

THOMAS SAMPSON OF KERSEY

Thomas was a rich peasant. In 1381 he owned:
- land in 3 villages
- 72 horses and cows
- part of a ship
- sheep and quite a bit of money.

Collector of the Poll Tax
In 1379 and 1381 Thomas collected the Poll Tax for the king.

Thomas rebels
In June 1381 he changed his mind. He led the peasants against the Poll Tax. In 1383 he was condemned to death. But he was pardoned.

LOWESTOFT ■

JOHN COLE

In 1363 John was fined for refusing to do winter work for his lord.

In 1381 he and others burnt some court records.

In 1384 he was fined for taking part in the Peasants' Revolt. But he argued with the court and did not pay the fine.

In 1385 John was accused of hitting another peasant.

Although he was supposed to be arrested, he is never heard of again.

Questions

1 Read **Where did the rebels come from?** From which 4 counties did the rebels come?

2 Read the box on **Adam Rogge**. Why do you think he joined the peasant rebels?

3 Read the box on **Thomas Sampson**. Why do you think he changed his mind about the Poll Tax?

The peasants march on London

On 12 June 1381, 60,000 peasants from Kent and Essex marched on London. They had hardly any real weapons. But they were determined.

Richard II goes down the river

King Richard II was only 14 years old. He decided to talk to the peasants.

Richard II, Simon Sudbury and Robert Hales set off in the royal barge to go down the river to meet the people.

Simon Sudbury and Robert Hales

These two men were advisers to Richard II. The peasants hated them. The peasants blamed them for the Poll Tax.

As soon as the peasants saw the two men, they shouted out that Sudbury and Hales were the traitors. They must be killed. Quickly the barge turned back.

The peasants are let into London

The people of London supported the peasants. They gave the peasants food. Then the peasants went on the rampage. They burnt the palace of the king's uncle. They burnt the building where legal records were kept.

Richard at the Tower

Richard II was safe in the Tower of London. The peasants rushed there and demanded to see him.

Source A

This painting shows Richard II meeting the peasants in June 1381.

Source B

Part of a speech made by John Ball to the peasants in 1381:

The men we call lords, what makes them our masters?

They live in fine houses. We sweat and work in the fields in wind and rain.

They call us slaves and beat us if we do not serve them.

We have no one to listen to us.

Let's go to the King and explain what it's like. Let's tell him we want it changed.

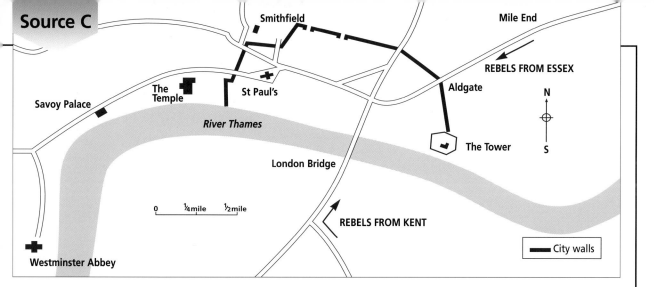

London in 1381 showing the routes the rebels took.

The King meets the peasants

Richard II met the peasants. The leader of the peasants was Wat Tyler. Wat Tyler asked Richard to do four things:

- end serfdom (no one has to stay working for the same lord)
- end labour services (no one has to work so many days a week for the lord for nothing)
- punish the king's advisers
- pardon all the peasants who had rebelled.

Richard agrees to all but one

Richard II would not punish his advisers. So the peasants killed them. They stuck the heads of Simon Sudbury and Robert Hales on poles.

The King meets the peasants again

This time Wat Tyler asked for more. Then no one is sure what happened. There was a scuffle and Wat Tyler fell dying. The peasants raised their bows, ready to fire. But Richard II rode forward. He said:

Would you shoot your king? I will be your leader. Follow me and you will have what you want.

He led them out of London. He persuaded them to go home.

Broken promises

As soon as he could, Richard II broke his promises to the peasants. Many were hanged or fined. Nothing changed.

Source D

Richard II said this to the peasants after the revolt. (A villein was a peasant who had to work for his lord.)

Villeins you were and villeins you shall remain.

Questions

1 Read **The King meets the peasants**.

 a Who was the leader of the peasants?

 b What four things did he ask for?

2 Read **Broken promises**. What happened to many of the peasants?

11.1 THE HUNDRED YEARS' WAR: EDWARD III AND THE BATTLE OF CRECY 1346

England and France quarrel about land

After 1066 English kings ruled land in France. The French did not like this. During King John's reign (1199–1216) they took most of the land back. The English did nothing about this until **Edward III** became king.

Why did the Hundred Years' War start?

1 Edward III said he was the rightful King of France.

ENGLAND
V
FRANCE

2 Edward III wanted land in France.

3 Edward III was angry because the French were helping the Scots to raid England.

4 Edward III enjoyed wars and fighting.

The English invade France

In 1337 Edward III invaded France. This started a long war which lasted until 1453. It is known as the Hundred Years' War.

What happened during the Hundred Years' War?

The English won a lot of battles to begin with. But the French fought back. By 1453 the English were left with just the port of Calais. The war cost a lot of money and many people were killed.

Source A

A modern picture of the types of people who went off to battle.

Cannon were used at the Battle of Crécy. Henry V had 75 gunners, who bombarded French towns.

As well as soldiers there were armourers, grooms, priests and doctors. Women joined as helpers.

Some bowmen also used crossbows. These were drawn by winding a handle, and could shoot arrows through armour.

A squire looked after a knight's armour, which packhorses carried. The squire helped the knight to put his armour on.

The Battle of Crécy, 1346

In 1346 Edward III sailed to France again. He had a big army and planned to capture Paris.

The English were chased by the French. They caught up with the English at Crécy. A battle took place.

Edward placed his army at the top of a hill. His men had time to eat and rest. The French had marched a long way and were tired.

The battle was fought on 26 August 1346. Source B tells you what happened.

Source B

Written by a French historian in 1401.

The French had crossbows.

The English had longbows.

It took longer to load a crossbow.

The King of France ordered his crossbowmen to march towards the English. The sun was in their eyes and they were tired.

The English archers fired their arrows. They went so quickly that they fell on the French like a heavy snowstorm. The crossbowmen ran away in panic.

Then English soldiers charged through the French. They had large knives. They killed many barons and knights. The French were beaten.

Questions

1 Look at page 84.
Which English king started the Hundred Years' War?

2 Read Source B.
Why did the English win Crécy?

Foot soldiers wore everyday clothes. They carried their own weapons.

English archers had longbows, which they carried wrapped in cloth. They wore leather **jerkins** and carried food in sacks.

A knight wore steel armour, as did his horse. He carried a shield and used an axe or mace to fight hand-to-hand.

Pages served the knights. They were sometimes killed helping knights off their horses during battle.

Henry V sails to France

On 11 August 1415, Henry V sailed to France. He had an army of 6,000 archers and 2,500 knights. Henry wanted to capture land from the French.

Henry V takes Harfleur

In September 1415 the English captured the town of Harfleur. Then came disaster. The Black Death broke out among the English. Many men died.

Henry was worried. He knew his army had been weakened.

The Battle of Agincourt, 25 October 1415

The French were waiting to fight Henry at the village of Agincourt.

Henry ordered his archers to walk towards the French. They got close and then fired a shower of arrows. Many French knights were killed. The English archers fired again and again.

Then the English fought the French with swords. More French soldiers were killed. Others ran from the battlefield. Henry had won a great victory.

Source A

A medieval painting of the Battle of Agincourt.

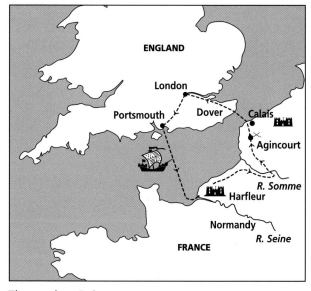

The road to Agincourt.

Battlefield doctors

There were many battles in medieval times. This meant doctors got a lot of practice in treating wounds.

Source B is a 'wound man'. It shows the wounds that doctors said they could heal. It also shows us the weapons used at the time.

Hugh of Lucca

Hugh was a doctor in Italy during the 1200s. He worked with the army in times of war.

He saw many different wounds. This forced him to try out different cures and treatments.

Hugh found out that wine would heal wounds. It helped to keep wounds clean. This was an important discovery.

But some doctors still used the old ointments that did not work.

Theodoric of Lucca

Theodoric was the son of Hugh. He was also an army doctor. He wrote about the ways of healing used by his father (Source C).

Henry V's doctors would have known about these treatments. They may well have used them at Agincourt.

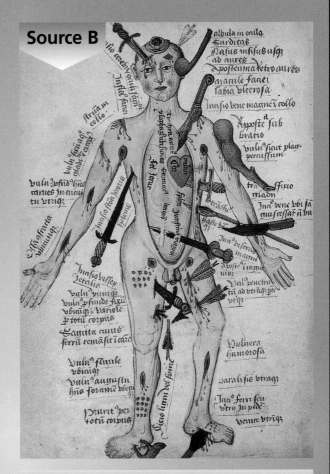

Source B

A medieval 'wound man'. It shows the wounds that army doctors could heal.

Source C

This was written by Theodoric of Lucca in 1267.

Every day new methods are being thought of for taking arrows out of a soldier. The army doctors are very clever.

My father used to heal most wounds with just wine. It worked very well. He did not use any ointments.

Questions

1. Look at Source B.
   Write down some of the wounds that doctors said they could cure.

2. Read **Battlefield doctors**.
   Why were army doctors good at treating wounds?

Henry VI of Lancaster

In 1422 Henry VI became the King of England. Henry was from a rich family called the House of Lancaster.

Henry was a weak king, who sometimes had fits of madness.

The House of York was another rich family in England. The York family hated Henry VI and said he was not fit to rule England.

The two families started to quarrel. They both wanted to rule England.

Source B

Ordinary people did not fight in the wars, but sometimes they were attacked by soldiers.

The Wars of the Roses

The Lancaster family wore a red rose as their badge. The York family wore a white rose.

The quarrel between the two families turned into a series of battles between 1454 and 1485.

These battles became known as the Wars of the Roses.

Both sides were rich enough to have their own private armies. The ordinary people of England did not fight in the battles. They went on with their lives as normal.

Source A

Lancastrians and Yorkists all descend from **Edward III** (1327–1377)

Key:
- Lancastrians
- Yorkists
- ✗ killed in battle
- 🗡 murdered

Richard Duke of York killed in 1461 ✗

Henry VI (1422–1461) (1470–1471) married Margaret of Anjou 🗡

Margaret Beaufort married Edmund Twdwr Earl of Richmond

Edward IV (1461–1483) formerly Earl of March married Elizabeth Woodville

Richard III (1483–1485) ✗

Elizabeth of York

Edward V (1483) died in Tower 1483 🗡

Richard died in Tower 1483 🗡

Edward Prince of Wales killed 1471 ✗

Henry VII (1485–1509) married Elizabeth of York

A family tree. It shows the families of York and Lancaster.

The Battle of Towton

Henry VI won the first battles. But in 1461 Henry was beaten by the York family at Towton in Yorkshire.
It was a fierce battle. Thousands were killed.

A river ran through the battlefield. It became blocked with dead bodies and the fields were flooded with blood.

Edward IV of York

After the Battle of Towton, Edward IV of York became king. He was a good soldier and much stronger than Henry VI.

More battles

Henry VI tried to win back the throne, but he was beaten by Edward IV in the battles of Barnet and Tewkesbury.

Murder?

In 1471 Henry VI died in the Tower of London. He was probably murdered on the orders of Edward IV.

Edward IV ruled until his death in 1483.

What would happen now?

The progress of the Wars of the Roses

1422–1461
Henry VI

1461–1471
Edward IV

1470–1471
Henry VI

1471–1483
Edward IV

1483
Edward V

1483–1485
Richard III

1485
Henry VII

End of the Wars of the Roses

The red boxes show Lancastrian kings, the white boxes show Yorkist kings. The dates shown are the years they reigned.

Questions

1 Read **Henry VI of Lancaster**.
Why did the York family and the Lancaster family quarrel?

2 Read **The Wars of the Roses**.
Why were the battles between the two families called the Wars of the Roses?

3 Read **The Wars of the Roses** and look at Source B.
What happened to ordinary people at this time?

Richard III – a wicked uncle?

Edward IV of York died in 1483. He left two sons:

1 Edward – aged 12.

2 Richard – aged 9.

Both princes were too young to rule England.

This job was given to their uncle – Richard, Duke of Gloucester.

He was a good soldier and was popular with many people.

Mystery

In July 1483, the Duke of Gloucester was crowned **Richard III**.

The two princes were living in the Tower of London. They were never seen again.

People began to say that Richard III had murdered them so that he could become the king.

Richard III lost some of his followers. They turned instead to support **Henry Tudor**, of the Lancaster family.

Bones

In 1674 the bones of two young boys were dug up in the Tower.

Some historians say that they are the bones of the princes; others disagree.

What really happened is still a mystery today.

Source A

Richard III, painted later.

Source B

Written by Sir Thomas More in 1520.

Sir James Tyrell was sent to the Tower with a letter from King Richard.

It said that he should be given all the keys of the Tower for the night.

That night the princes were smothered while they were asleep.

Sir James rode to tell King Richard. He was very pleased.

Henry Tudor

In 1485 Henry Tudor of Lancaster landed in Wales. He had been living in France for his own safety for a number of years.

He was going to win the throne from Richard III.

He marched into England.

People joined his army on the way. He soon had an army of 5,000 men.

The Battle of Bosworth Field 1485

Henry Tudor fought Richard III at Bosworth Field.

Although he had a bigger army, Richard III was beaten. The battle was all over in less than an hour.

Richard was cut down and killed.

There is a story that Richard's crown was found in a thorn bush and given to Henry.

He became Henry VII, the first Tudor king.

The Tudor rose

In 1486 Henry VII married **Elizabeth of York**.

He did this to show that the Wars of the Roses were over.

The white rose of York and the red rose of Lancaster were made into one rose.

The new rose was called the Tudor rose. It was red on the outside and white in the middle.

The Tudor rose. It is a double rose: red on the outside and white in the middle.

Questions

1 Read **Mystery**.
 Why might Richard III have murdered the princes?

2 Read **The Battle of Bosworth Field 1485**.
 What happened at this battle?

3 Read **The Tudor rose**.
 What did Henry VII do to show that the Wars of the Roses were over?

bailey castle wall surrounding the castle courtyard.

charter the rules about governing the country or a city, agreed between the king and the people and written down.

crusade journey by Christian soldiers to fight the Muslims for control of Jerusalem.

crusaders Christian soldiers who set off to rescue Jerusalem from the Muslims.

Domesday Book this contained all the information collected for William the Conqueror about the size of English villages and farms.

fealty a promise of obedience sworn by the nobles to the king.

feudal system the way people were organised into fighting for the nobles and the king in return for having some land.

guild a 'club' for craftsmen and merchants which looked after them and made sure their work was good. Each craft had its own guild.

infidels people who were not Christians.

jerkin a leather jacket with no sleeves.

keep a high tower inside a castle.

Magna Carta the 'Great Charter' the nobles made King John agree to. It was a list of things that would give the **nobles** more power.

mayor the leader of a town, chosen by the townspeople.

merchants people who bought goods from one person and sold them to another.

monasteries the buildings where monks lived and worked.

monk a man who gives up ordinary life to pray and work for God and live in a **monastery**.

motte the mound of earth where a castle is built.

nobles the few most important men in the country next to the king. Usually knights or lords, they were rich and powerful.

Normans the French men who came over to England with William the Conqueror in 1066. They settled in England.

nun a woman who gives up ordinary life to pray and work for God and live in a **nunnery**.

nunneries the buildings where **nuns** lived and worked.

packhorses horses used for carrying luggage.

pilgrimage a journey to a holy place, usually for a special religious reason.

poultice a warm bandage wrapped on a swelling or boil to make it go down.

reeve the person in charge of the farms and the villages belonging to a lord.

relic part of a holy person kept after they have died. The relic was believed to have special powers - even of curing illness.

Rule of St Benedict a set of rules made by St Benedict for **monks** to follow throughout their lives.

Acre, Siege of 40–1

Ball, John 78–9, 82
barons 36–7
Battle of:
  Agincourt (1415) 86
  Bannockburn (1314) 61
  Bosworth Field (1485) 91
  Crécy (1346) 85
  Hastings (1066) 10–11, 14
  Towton (1461) 89
Bayeux Tapestry 9, 11,
  12, 17
Becket, Thomas
  (Archbishop of
  Canterbury) 34–5
Black Death (plague)
  70–5, 86
  how it started 70–1
  no cure for 72–3
  results of 78–9
  in France 76
  in Italy 76
  in England 77
Bruce, Robert
  (of Scotland) 61

Canterbury 35
castles 12, 16–17, 31, 33,
  158–9
children 51
country life 44–7, 50–1
  on the manor 48–9
  (see also Black Death,
  Peasants' Revolt)
crusades 38–43
  and Siege of Acre 40–1

David II (King of Scotland)
  60
Domesday Book 14
doctors (see Medicine)

Earls 5, 6, 9, 13–15, 30–1,
  33, 34
Edward the Confessor 8–9
Edward I (King of England)
  58–9, 62–3
Edward II (King of
  England) 61
Edward III (King of
  England) 60
  and Hundred Years' War
  84–5
Edward IV (King of
  England) 89
Eleanor of Aquitaine
  (Queen of England) 37
  farming 5, 44–5, 46–7,
  48–9, 74–5
fealty 54, 56, 60
feudal system 14
food and drink 40, 50, 62,
  65, 68, 69
France 7
  and Hundred Years' War
  84–5
guilds 65

Harald Hardrada (King of
  Norway) 8–9
Harold Godwinson 8–11
Henry I (King of England)
  30–1
Henry II (King of England)
  6, 32–3, 34–5, 36, 56–7
Henry V (King of England)
  86–7
Henry VII (King of England)
  90–1
homes 3, 49, 63, 68–9
Hundred Years' War 7, 84–5

infidels 19
Ireland 54, 55, 56–7

Jerusalem 19, 22, 38
John (King of England) 6,
  36–7, 43, 44
Julian of Norwich 28

lavatories 49, 63, 68
law and order:
  Church courts 34–5
  manor courts 52–3, 80, 81
  royal courts 30, 33, 52–3
  punishments 52-3, 58,
  80–1
Llewelyn ap Gryffyd
  (Welsh ruler) 58
London 62–3

McMurrough, Dermot 56–7
Magna Carta 7, 36–7
Matilda (Queen of England)
  30–1, 33
medicine 22, 43, 68, 72, 87
merchants 66–7
monks (see religion,
  Fountains Abbey)
Muslims 38–43

nobles (see Earls)
Normans 10, 12–15, 57
nuns 28–29

Peasants' Revolt 78–83
Plague (see Black Death)
Poll Tax (1377, 1379,
  1381) 79
Princes in the Tower 90

religion 7, 18–19
  Christendom 18
  Church and Government
  6, 18–21, 34–5
  Church courts 34–5
  churches, abbeys and

cathedrals 5, 7, 18, 21, 24–5
holy days 23, 101
monks 24–7, 28
nuns 28–9
pilgrimages 22
Pope 6, 18, 20, 34
prayer 4, 5, 7
priests 20–1, 45, 46
relics 22
Richard I (King of England) 40, 42–3
Richard II (King of England) 82–3
Richard III (King of England) 90–1

St Benedict 24, 27
Saladin (Muslim leader) 39
Scotland 60–1
social organisation 5, 14, 20, 44–5, 46, 78
Statute of Labourers (1351) 78
Stephen (King of England) 30–1, 33
Stone of Scone 60
Strongbow 47

taxes 21, 22, 36–7, 43, 64, 78–9, 82
toilets *see* lavatories
town life 62–3, 68–9
  and charters 64
  trade 66–7
  (*see* also guilds)
trade 64–5, 66–7
Tudors (*see* Henry VII)
Tudor Rose 91
Tyler, Wat 79, 83

Vikings 15
village life 44–5, 50–1
  and crime 52–3

Wales 54–5, 58
war:
  civil war 31, 37
  with France 84–5
  Ireland 54–7
  Scotland 60–1
  Wales 58
  (see also Battles, crusades)
Wars of the Roses 88–9
William the Conqueror (Duke of Normandy) 8–11, 12–15, 58, 60, 62
wool trade 64
women 4, 28–9, 31, 37, 47, 64, 68–9

Acknowledgements

The authors and publishers would like to thank the following for permission to reproduce photographs:

Aerofilms Ltd: 1.1D
Ancient Art and Architecture: 3.1B
Bibliothèque Nationale, Paris/Bridgeman Art Library: 5.2B, 9.4D, 10.3A
Bibliothèque Royale de Belgique/Bridgeman Art Library: 8.3B
Bibliothèque Royale Albert: 9.1A
Bodleian Library: 2.4A, 3.3B, 3.5A
British Library: 1.1F, 3.4A, 3.5B, 3.6A, 5.3A, 6.1A, 6.2A, 6.4A, 8.1A, 8.2B, 9.2B 6.5A
British Library/Bridgeman Art Library: 3.6B, 4.3A, 8.2D, 10.1B
Masters and Fellows of Corpus Christi College, Cambridge: 1.1E
English Heritage: 2.2A, 3.4D
Giraudon/Bridgeman Art Library: 1.1A
Michael Holford: 2.1A, 2.2B, 2.3A
House of Commons/Bridgeman Art Library: 4.4A
A K Kersting: 3.1A
Lambeth Palace Library/Bridgeman Art Library: 11.2A
Museum of London: 3.3B
National Museum of Ireland: 7.2A
National Portrait Gallery: 11.4A
The National Trust Photographic Library: 3.4E
Scottish National Portrait Gallery: 7.4C
St Mary's Church, North Mimms: 3.2
Trinity College, Dublin: 7.2B
Wellcome Institute Library: 11.2B

The publishers have made every effort to trace copyright holders of material in this book. Any omissions will be rectified in subsequent printings if notice is given to the publisher.

The authors and publishers gratefully acknowledge the following publications from which written sources in the book are drawn. In some sources the wording or sentence structure has been simplified.

W Anderson (ed. trans.), *Chronicles*, Centaur Press, 1963: 11.1B
Camden Society XXXVII, *A Relation of the Island of England, in about the year 1500*, 1847: 6.5B
John Chancellor, *Edward I*, Weidenfeld and Nicholson, 1981: 7.3A
Geoffrey Chaucer, *The Canterbury Tales*, Penguin, 1962: 3.3A
Ian Ferguson, *History of the Scots*, Oliver and Boyd, 1987: 7.4A
G N Garmonsway (trans.), *The Anglo-Saxon Chronicle*, Dent, 1972: 4.1
W O Hassal, *They saw it Happen 55 BC – 1485*, Blackwell, 1965: 4.3B, 11.4B

Robert Higham and Philip Barker, *Timber Castles*, B T Batsford, 1992: 2.5D
Rosemary Horrocks, *The Black Death*, Manchester University Press, 1994: 9.1C, 9.2A, 9.4A, 9.4B, 9.4E, 9.4F
E M C van Houts, 'The Norman Conquest through European Eyes', *English Historical Review*, 110, 1995: 2.5B
John Joliffe (trans.) *Froissart's Chronicles*, Harville Press, London, 1967: 1.1C, 10.3B
E D Kirk (ed. trans.), *Piers Plowman*, WW Norton, 1990: 10.1A
Tony McAleavy, *Conflict in Ireland*, Holmes McDougal, 1987: 7.2A
Sir Hugh Middleton, *Historical Pamphlets No.4*, Order of St John of Jerusalem, Library Committee, 1930: 3.4C
C Platt, *The English Medieval Town*, Paladin, 1976: 8.2A, 8.2C, 10.1C
Eileen Power, *Medieval Women*, Methuen, 1975: 3.6C
E Revell (ed.) *Later Letters of Peter of Blois*, OUP, 1993: 4.2B
H T Riley (ed.) *Thomae Walsingham Historia Anglicana* in part one of *Chronica Monasterii Sancti Albani*, Rolls Series, 1863-4: 10.3D
Schools Council Project, *Medicine through Time*, Book 3: 8.1B, 11.2C
E Woelfflin (ed. trans.), *Regula Monachorum*, Lipsiae, 1895: 3.4B

Reed Educational and Professional Publishing Ltd
Halley Court, Jordan Hill, Oxford OX2 8EJ

MELBOURNE AUCKLAND FLORENCE PRAGUE MADRID ATHENS SINGAPORE TOKYO SAO PAULO CHICAGO PORTSMOUTH NH MEXICO IBADAN GABORONE JOHANNESBURG KAMPALA NAIROBI

© Fiona Reynoldson and David Taylor 1997

The moral rights of the proprietors have been asserted.

First published 1997

00 99 98 97
10 9 8 7 6 5 4 3 2 1

British Library Cataloguing in Publication Data is available from the British Library on request.

ISBN 0435 309 536

Designed and produced by Dennis Fairey and Associates Ltd

Illustrated by Richard Berridge, Finbarr O' Connor, John James, Angus McBride, Arthur Phillips, Piers Sanford and Stephen Wisdom.

Printed in Hong Kong by Wing King Tong Co. Ltd.

Cover design by Wooden Ark

Cover photograph: *Massacre of Rebellious French Peasants at Meaux 1358*, Courtesy of e.t. archive.